# An Irish Tale of Leaving

Darrell Duke

## Stagehead Publishing

Newfoundland

**Library and Archives Canada Cataloguing in Publication**

Duke, Darrell, 1970 -, author

An Irish Tale of Leaving/Darrell Duke

First Canadian Edition/Issued in print and electronic formats

ISBN-13: 978-1986674157

Rebels in Ireland—Aran Islands—Galway Bay—Newfoundland and Labrador—Argentia—Placentia Bay—History—18th century. 2. Irish Emigration—Early Settlers of Newfoundland—History— Marquise--Placentia Bay (NL)—18th century.

### © 2018 by Darrell Duke

Printed in the USA

Cover Inspiration by Jessica Duke

Cover Design by Emma Duke

### Stagehead Publishing
243 Marine Drive, Clarenville, NL, A5A 1M9
www.darrellduke.com

This book is dedicated to the loving memory of my father, Gerry Duke, and to my mother, Shirley, whose belief in my abilities as an author and musician inspire me to continue writing and performing.

Dad, your untimely death has left a void too large to fill with mere words. Your beautiful, gentle soul will guide me throughout the remainder of my journey here, dreams included. I miss you so much. Mama, thank you for your love and support. I will always love you both.

# PREFACE

My Grandfather, James Houlihan, was from the community of Argentia, once known as Little Placentia, located on the western side of Newfoundland's Placentia Bay. His father, Edward, and his father, James, were also from there. My Great, Great, Great, Grandfather, also James, was conceived in Ireland and born at Cooper's Cove, Marquise, just across the sheltered harbour from Little Placentia. His father, my fourth Great Grandfather, Edward "Red" Houlihan, was from Ireland.

When I first read the line, "The musket ball hitting her sounded like the slap of a hand on the back," I was hooked. Those were the words of Red Houlihan transcribed to paper by his great grandson, John G. Houlihan, sometime in the late 1800s. Without John G's efforts (taking the time and effort to jot down the oral tales of Red Houlihan) it's highly unlikely I would have done more than pencil a sad song from scanty stories, had they survived.

Through much research by my cousin, Ed Ginn of New Jersey, members of our family first received this vital ancestral history circa 1990. Ed's mother, Florence Houlihan Ginn, was my Grandfather's sister who'd migrated from Argentia to The States as a young woman. In 2006, I received a copy of Red's family tree from Mary Bradbury whose grandmother was a Houlihan from Little Placentia. In 2012, my Aunt Bernie (Houlihan) O'Reilly gave me an envelope containing the aforementioned quote and other golden information. I am indebted to all of these people for generating and reinforcing my interest in this truly intense and interesting story.

Red Houlihan was born on such a magnificent chunk of rock that Newfoundlanders might struggle to consider it prideworthy to call Newfoundland The Rock. Red's rock is called Inis Meáin, anglicized as Inishmaan or 'Middle Island.' It is one of the Oileáin Árann (Aran Islands), located in Galway Bay, on Ireland's west coast. To the north of Inis Meáin is Árainn Mhór (mór 'big'). It has been anglicized as Aranmore or Arranmore. The third, and smallest of the three islands, is Inis Oirthir ('Island of the East') and the recognized form Inis Oírr has been anglicized to Inisheer.

In 2005, in Galway, I sat in a meadow near an ancient round tower, looking out at the bay and its long slabs of rock - the Aran Islands. From that view, I couldn't imagine anyone, or anything, for that matter, living on such windswept, water-torn, cold heaps of stone. It wasn't until I read the information given by Aunt Bernie that I realized what I'd captured seven years earlier on camera - the birthplace of my Mother's side of the family, the Houlihans.

I then read J.M. Synge's The Aran Islands (1907) which paints great images of the landscape where my people once lived, worked, hid, prayed and played. To fathom they spoke another language is near impossible to grasp. To know I speak English because my forbearers were no longer allowed to converse in their native tongue, Gaelic, or simply Irish, can sometimes be more bitter than sweet.

Having learned of tragedies endured by Red Houlihan, the loss of a language may seem small. But, really, it was no diminutive ingredient in forcing him from his homeland. Like multiple thousands of other young Irishmen, Red was part of a group known as Rebels who rejected the tyranny of England's militant leaders sent to Ireland to impose strict laws over every aspect of Irish people and their lives. By 1778, the English had been in Ireland, in one form or another, for almost six-hundred years. Red's wife was shot in cold blood by British soldiers, or Peelers, as the locals called them. Peelers called the likes of Red Houlihan and his comrades-in-arms Rebels.

I am aware that many of today's natives of Ireland find it absurd to speak of atrocities committed by Great Britain in Ireland so long ago and, in the name of moving forward, I respect that. On that note, I consider this book a form of personal closure on ancient resentments passed down through the generations.

This book is not intended as a complete history of Little Placentia/Argentia, Marquise, Newfoundland, Ireland, the American Revolution, nor England's positions in Ireland's past. It is a story of a man, Red Houlihan, his life in Ireland, and his departure from his homeland to Newfoundland in the 18th Century.

DARRELL DUKE

# CHAPTER ONE

## *Newfoundland, 1808*

Red Houlihan runs through the opaque woods covering the hills of Marquise. The needles of spruce tree branches prick his face. The enemy isn't far behind. Heavy boots snap dry, fallen sticks. The crackling noises in the otherwise still of night send echoes to Red's ears. He considers falling to one side or the other, or dropping to his knees and rolling, should a gun be fired. The blackthorn walking stick gripped tightly in his left hand is bit of a hindrance amongst the dense forest, but he can hardly let it go. It had saved him many times in the past and it will, no doubt, get him out of this and other scrapes to follow. If he can situate himself properly, that is. The pleurisy is back. The uncomfortable sensation. Subtle pain beneath the strained muscles in the right side of his chest is bothersome. It is accompanied by a weariness fit to kill him if he doesn't soon stop and rest.

Shouts of orders to halt or they'll shoot reach Red's ears. The enemies' voices reverberate all around the rocky terrain just beyond both sides of the forest. In an accent he was taught to hate since birth comes the word *Ribbonism*. It sounds stridently in his head. The word invokes memories. Too many at once to focus on. A weight his mind can do without.

Red leaps over a four-foot embankment, a place from where he regularly digs black earth for his vegetable garden and where juicy worms to lure big trout to the hook of his fishing line keep out of the sun. He runs into a perpendicular rock, twists his body and turns. He lands on a flat stone and rolls off the big rock. His foot catches in an exposed tree root. Struggling to raise his arms above his head, Red stretches to help ease the strained muscles of his back. He winces from the pain in his ankle, but remains silent for fear of alerting the ensuing soldiers, telling of his whereabouts.

With his good arm, Red drags himself back over the rock, into the dug-out bank. He hopes the enemy will run on by, not notice him. Give him a chance to take the old path closer to the harbour where he can get back to his house and grab his gun before they spot him again. And shoot. He'd never consider firing on an unarmed person, but the British don't have a problem with it, he knows well. For the few seconds it takes to wonder why he'd left his gun behind before heading off into the hills this morning, he lifts his head.

"There he is!" a soldier shouts. "Stop Whiteboy, so we may find a suitable tree to hang your revolting head; let the dogs eat of you what we decide not to shred."

Red hears poetry in what's just been said, but highly doubts it was intentional. Or maybe they are mocking him and his people - the Irish - a people of multiple backgrounds, infamous for their instinctive literary proclivities.

Red ignores the hate-filled voices. The chase picks up where it left off. He runs like mad through a meadow, down towards the harbour. The ankle injury is agonizing. He heads into a droke of trees for cover before the enemies take aim with their muskets and fire. But he isn't quick enough.

Red hears the crackling of musket fire. Then feels a lead ball enter his skin. The sulfuric stench of gun powder, like rotten eggs, is carried quickly on the wind, engulfing Red's sense of smell. The stink, invoking a lifetime of horrid memories, cascades his being. The surge of loathing racing through his body instills in him the sense he could leap a hundred feet in the air to outrun his would-be capturers. Or turn back and pounce on them like ants. Intruders. Enemies. But it's too late. He grabs the branch of a tree for support. The hot metal stings, having torn open the skin of his lower back. He falls to his knees and tries to raise both hands above his head in surrender. His right shoulder is weak from an old injury and the pain of trying to raise that arm excruciating. Numbness sets over his hips and thighs. Blood from the wound runs around his waist, down over his groin and upper legs. It's scalding hot. Then cold.

Across the vast bay the sallow, full moon soars above Red Island. The white sails of a tall ship reflect the cosmological light, as the vessel leans slightly into the wind. The black water of the sea shimmers splendidly in the creased pathway painted by the moon. Red fades in and out of consciousness.

Not knowing whether the soldiers will finish him off or try and take him hostage, he lets out a scream heard for miles. He audibly invites death to take him; finally, a demise he feels will at last bring peace. Voices from behind become louder, clearer. There is a tone of fear, but not without a tinge of amusement. The bastards are mocking him again.

"I shoulda killed ye all, every last one o' ye, when I'd the chance," Red says, as if he were given an opportunity to say a few words before he dies.

"Ya okay there, Mr. Houlihan?" a young man's voice asks.

The accent isn't English.

"Anudder traitor is what we have here, is it?" Red demands to know.

But the resignation of defeat in his voice overrides his efforts at true seriousness. He doesn't care anymore.

Snickers from one of the soldiers makes another angry.

"Ah, b'y, give it up, will ya? He's been through enough, can't ya tell!"

*These can't be British soldiers*, Red thinks.

He turns his head slowly toward his company. Recoiling from the ache of his swollen ankle, he's scared to move for fear of forcing more blood from the open wound in his back. Slowly, he drops his left arm. The right one has already fallen limp by his side. Fleeting clouds move on, cautiously giving the fair moon back to the unblemished night sky. The black shadows before Red turn into trees and rocks and bushes, and the bright light he'd accepted as Heaven only moments before vanishes behind a muddle of clouds again. Disappointment in being alive shrouds him once more, until he hears a young man's voice.

"Mr. Houlihan? 'Tis alright. There's no one here t' bother ya, just a few of us lads out gallivantin'. We're terribly sorry fer yer great loss, sir."

The old man knows the voice, one of the Hunt boys from down by the Shag Pond. Red drinks with the boy's father most Saturday nights. They've been friends a lifetime.

Red looks forward, and then side to side, making sure he isn't being set up. Slowly, he turns his head.

"Goddamn it, Andy!" he says. "I broke me bottle."

Andy Hunt and his buddies laugh, mostly out of relief that Red Houlihan is back from wherever he'd been in his mind. The blood soaking Red's dungarees isn't blood at all, but poteen from the broken liquor bottle in his arse pocket.

4

"I'd offer ye a drop, me b'ys, but it appears there's none left," he says, offering a little laugh to rid the tension he's sure he has caused.

The lads begin to go on their way, knowing old Red will find his way back to his home down across the meadow. They've heard bits and pieces, alternate versions of his story. Everyone in the area feels they know about the same. Episodes like this have been occurring since Red first arrived here twenty-five years ago. Stories of his wild escapades are as familiar as the landscape. These young men also know they, or anyone one else, won't lay eyes on Red Houlihan again for a while. And if he does budge from his home, he won't speak to a soul for weeks on end. No one judges him; at least, not to his face, for his existence prior to coming to Newfoundland was far from enchanting. That much, they know. For it was young Andy Hunt's father, Red's old companion from Galway, who'd invited Red to Little Placentia in the first place.

"T'day 'twas the hardest I've had here yet, b'ys." He says. "Buryin' yer own child is never aisey. No matter how old they lives t' be. I hope ye never has t' face the like."

"We got a drop, Mr. Houlihan, if ya please," young Andy Hunt says, having changed his mind about leaving.

"Oi," Red said, reaching up for the bottle in Andy's hand. *"Go raibh maith agaibh."*

"Yer welcome, Sir," Andy answers.

The young men sit in the soft, cold grass and lean against large rocks and tree trunks. The aroma of grass is sweet and soothing. So is the smell of salt cod in piles surrounding both sides of the harbour. The fish awaits the ever-hopeful prospect of the sun bursting through the next morning's sure fog so the fish may be laid out again to continue drying.

The drink, made from potatoes, is potent. It quickly gives the lads courage to attempt finding out more about Red Houlihan's past.

Red takes another big swig of the alcohol before passing it to the nearest fellow. He places his massive hands over the fire made by a couple of the young men. Their pinched, orange faces change shape with the shadows cast by the fire's light. Light gusts of wind comb gently the thick grass of the meadow. Red reaches warily behind his back. One of the young men flinches. Red's eyebrows furrow and he shakes his head.

"What's the matter, sir?" Andy asks. "Are ya cut?"

"Nah, nah," Red says. "Strange enough, I've ne'er cut. *Feadóg stain.*"

"Ah, what Sir?" one of the nervous lads asks.

"Me whistle!" Red snaps. "I lost me whistle."

One of the young men quickly takes a torch from the fire and wanders up the grade, toward the embankment where Red says he'd tumbled earlier. The young man keeps the burning stick close to the ground, squinting into the uncut grass.

"Not wurt' burnin' the place down fer, lad!" Red growls.

"I have it," the young man soon calls out, and he returns to the fireside with the whistle.

"*Go raibh maith agat,*" Red says in the softest voice heard from him tonight.

"What'd he say?" the young man who'd found the whistle asks.

"T'anks," answers Andy. "He said t'ank you."

"You were in the States too long, b'y," another torments.

"After a lifetime of not bein' allowed t' use our own talk at home," the young man feels a need to explain, "by the time we got t' Amerikay, Mammy an' Da were 'fraid t' speak the Irish, so I never heared much of it growin' up. Sorry, Mr. Houlihan."

"*Ná bíodh imní ort,*" Red says seriously, then smirks at the lad. "Don't worry."

They all laugh, as Red ruffles the young man's hair.

"*Éist le do chroí,*" Red says.

"What'd he say?" the Irish-American boy whispers.

"Listen t' yer heart," another says.

For almost five minutes the young men are lost in the reeling notes of the wooden whistle dangling from the mouth of the old man. His reddish-brown and graying beard runs all the way down behind the whistle. The coarse copper hairs of Red's beard glisten in the fire's light. The crackling of burning wood only enhances the music. Red's sleeves are rolled to his elbows and the sight of the width of his muscular forearms adds to the tension-filled moments. The full moon slips aside from its murky blanket of cloud again, lending a false sense of warmth against the gusts of wind having shifted. From the northeast now, they blow colder. The fire is left to die.

The red gemstone in the ring on Red's little finger catches the moon's bright light, as if on cue from the haunting tremolo of each note blown. The ring belonged to his father and wearing it had always given Red a sense of comfort in an often senseless world. The tune has an almost march-like quality to it. A deep sense of loss is borne with the nimble whir of the fresh wind. The last note Red blows is drawn-out. Low. From behind his closed eyes come tears. They disappear beneath the big beard clinging to his sunken cheeks and soak into his worn woolen sweater. *Never hesitate*, he hears his father's voice anchored deeply, sturdily in the back of his mind. For a moment the wind stirring his head of curls on the back of an otherwise bald head comes off Galway Bay, across the wide beach of Inis Meáin, over the island's patchwork of stone fences and in through the open door of his childhood home.

His eyes open to reveal a soul far flung from this moment. A couple of the young men tense at the sight. Red's pupils are big and black, like those of a frightened cat. He stares into the orange, blue and purple hues of the fire's weakening flames huddling against blackened rocks. The tone in Red's voice becomes that of a much younger man. Less frantic than what people here are used to. He's calm. Almost too calm. Uneasiness returns to a few of the young men. Coughing lightly, one of them tries warily to rupture the old man's spell. At the risk of an outburst from Red, the young man dares to speak.

"What? What happened, Sir?"

Red's pupils dilate again. The whites of his eyes veiled somewhere in a terror and odium impossible to disguise. Tension amongst his young company deepens yet again. Twirling the whistle slowly between his fingers, Red closes one eye and gazes through the hollow of the instrument with the other. The last embers of burning wood barely highlight the surrounding rocks.

"Sir?"

From its sleep, a crow caws, further startling the young men. Shivers travel down their spines while they await something, anything, from Red. His eyes are closed, his head tilted as though he, too, is awaiting inspiration or permission from some unforeseen force for his old life to unfold once more. He couldn't care less, but the boys sense another outburst and are unsure of what they'll have to do to avoid it.

The crow sounds again, less starling to the humans this time, but no less aggravated over the interruption to its sleep. Silhouetted against the returned moon, its wings swish the cold night air. With two complete turns, it circles above the droke of trees partially shading the boys and Red from the dense dampness of nighttime. The crow then flies off to where it might find a quieter place of rest.

"Mr. Houlihan?" young Andy Hunt tries to get a reaction, or better yet a story, from the weary old man.

At last, following a deep breath, Red speaks.

"'Touch an' go,'" said I. Touch an' go,'" Red shouts. His voice carries for miles around the meadows, hills and coves of Marquise and across the water to Little Placentia. "An' wit' that, I dug me spurs into the horse's belly, an' we left the peelers far behind."

DARRELL DUKE

# CHAPTER TWO

## *Ireland, 1778*

For all Red Houlihan knows, the British soldiers are dead. At least, that's what he hopes.

For his involvement with several cells of civilian groups raging against British rule, especially the Penal Laws, Red knows if he stops, he's a dead man. They'll all be killed. Maybe not right away. But soon enough.

After a few days in Galway gaol, they'll be hanged, along with dozens of others who've stood for the simple belief in their right to live in peace. To practice their Catholic faith. To reclaim their ancestors' land. To live free of unjust rents to absentee landlords and tithes to a Church not their own. And to speak, sing and pray in their native Irish tongue. But the Brits will have none of that. Sustained ill treatment of every conceivable notion is what the enemy has in mind for the slaves they've long since made of Ireland's people. No secret is made of that.

Red has been squealed on by a traitor, maybe more than one. Armed British soldiers have been sent to stand in his way on a long path leading from the Longford Mountains into Galway. It's a rougher than usual terrain Red takes when traveling to meetings in caves beneath waterfalls and ancient, abandoned bastion remains in Ireland's massive interior. The enemy is keen to take the Rebel alive, to torture him before a hanging or deport him to a far-away land called New Holland - an idea designed to colonize a foreign land in the Southern Hemisphere still in deep discussion behind parliament doors in London.

The soldiers choose not to fire upon Red, his wife and their young son as they advance on their family horse. Red takes advantage of the soldiers' hesitation and semi-lowered weapons to trample the three soldiers with the horse before speeding away.

Four days prior, Red had negotiated a ride on a hooker from his Inis Meáin home. They sailed the twenty-five miles in through Galway Bay before tying up at Galway's main, old pier. Though he'd done it many times, he felt the ten-mile row to Doolin in Claire in his canvas currach too risky. The sea, especially the tides of False Bay, is treacherous at best. Making good headway is always priority.

This time, the meeting was set to be held in Cavan. It was farther than Red usually travelled, and he couldn't afford a fight with the sea. Chance being late. At the gathering, there was much to discuss. To figure out. To learn. Young boys, scouts, had done their work. They are from Ireland's east, west, and south coast brigades of ordinary men carrying the need for retribution handed them by their fathers and grandfathers. Scouts found out where British troops were and at which times, and how many of them. They then reported the details to the elders, and burgeoning leaders, like Red, who'd bring the informant's particulars to the big meeting.

The other route for Red from Inis Meáin is an almost thirteen-mile stretch of equally-rough water to Ros a' Mhíl in Galway. This was out of the question. Extra British troops are stationed near there, right in the way of what would otherwise be an undisturbed, eastward hike to the city. Red's horse and weapons awaited him in hiding at a relative's place, his Aunt Máire's. Her home and out-buildings stand on a property enclosed with ancient trees. According to British law, it is situated the proper number of miles for a Catholic to reside outside a city.

Red let on he was a full-time fisherman from the hooker and stuck around the long, narrow boat working like a dog until all supplies and fish were offloaded to pay for his voyage. He kept his head down, out of direct eye contact with a pair of tired soldiers supposedly maintaining account of comings and goings in the harbour. Without hesitation, Red slung fish into woven baskets and lugged them up a ladder to the top of the wharf. He'd give his hands a good scrubbing before having a smoke.

This method of arriving in Galway might be a bit riskier, but it's easier than trying to land a small boat in Doolin. The walk from there to the city usually takes Red eight or nine hours. There'd be plenty of time for that. On long days and evenings with Ellen, when they could spare time for making love and plans near Listoonvarna, Kilmoon, and Ballyvaughan. The cavernous valleys provide protection from all human eyes and most ears. Red trembled at the thought of holding his lovely wife again.

Red stands by the Spanish Arch. Bare-footed women and young girls are selling fish. Herring, mostly. Red stares at a section of the arch destroyed by a tsunami twenty-three years earlier - a far-reaching effect of the 1755 Lisbon Earthquake in the Kingdom of Portugal where, there alone, tens of thousands of people perished. Red walks over to a boat belonging to a couple of brothers he knows from Galway. His hands now clean, he asks permission and goes below. Out of the wind now, he lifts the flue from a lit lantern and takes a piece of dry reed from his pocket. Igniting the reed from the flame, he quickly lights his pipe. One day, when he can afford it, he'll own one of those tinder boxes with the steel and flint. Then he won't have to waste time bothering people for a light.

"T'anks, gentlemen," Red offers, as he climbs back onto the pier.

He heads back to the Arch. Before taking the next big drag

on his pipe, Red looks around. The smell of smoldering tobacco leaves soothes him. It reminds him of peaceful nights at home on the island. His father telling stories and singing rhymes of old. The Spanish Arch, once an extension of the city wall, was made to protect the city's quays here in the Fish Market - from Martin's Tower to the banks of the Gaillimh, the three and a half-mile-long river running from Lough Corrib through Galway until it meets the sea.

In the reflection of the sky, dark clouds gather. Red pretends to be interested in the fish swimming in every direction beneath ravenous, gliding swans. He ponders how he can best use the next forty-eight hours. His eyes scour the water and the fortress-like city. What he can see of it. His thoughts work through ideas he'll soon present to his comrades-in-arms at the meeting. This one is to be held a mile or so from Coote Hill, a market town in Cavan. Two days' time. Flecks of rain darken the dust on Red's exposed, large forearms and he moves closer to the nearly two-hundred-year-old wall.

In the five or so years since his father was slain, Red has grown from a slim teenager into a robust man of twenty-one. He doubts any soldiers would notice him. Especially with the big beard covering much of his angular, grave face. There's an air of comfort in that. Incognito. Of being able to move freely about. Carry out his plans without drawing suspicion.

Red takes another drag on his pipe until the remaining tobacco turns to ashes. He closes his eyes and holds the smoke in his lungs as long as he can. Opening his eyes, he exhales the smoke to the gathering wind now warping the water's reflection of the disconsolate sky. Swans voice annoyance at the ripples interrupting their once-perfect scope of meals below. Red taps his clay pipe on the old wall, sending ashes to the soft, damp ground. He shoves the pipe into a pocket of his black, newly-knitted coat, and adjusts the dark, woolen cap covering his big ears. He hauls it down on all sides until he feels warmer.

Red longs for Ellen and John, his wife and child. The pit of loneliness in his stomach deepens. He feels like vomiting. At least the awful feeling will be quelled once they're reunited. Unlike the soreness in his soul born of the reality he'll never again see his father nor feel his strong embrace. Red always knew theirs was a special bond, his and his father's. Da. His thoughts cast elsewhere - to the ocean and its opus of reverberations from all the thrusting and heaving of water upon the land. The swirling and chattering balks of gulls covet the top of the stone wall enclosing much of the inner harbour. Moving clouds veil the sun. Looking in the opposite direction, a warmth arises within Red. It's in those far-off hills of green and brown where he'll soon find his waiting family.

After a couple of quick drinks with old friends, Red relaxes a little. Walking casually to double-check his buddy's boat, he ensures it is secure at its moorings amongst the other hookers lining the quay. Swans continue to wade gracefully, in spite of the windswept surface of the sheltered harbour. The beautiful birds extend their long necks for the few crumbs of an oatcake Red dares to spare before taking a nibble himself.

A while later, outside the walls of the old city, Red kneels at the edge of the *Gaillimh* (Stoney) River from which Galway received its name. Legend of the *Gaillimh* says it was named for Gaillimh inion Breasail, daughter of a Fir Bolg chieftain who'd drowned in the river. Through his wooden whistle, Red softly blows a tune. He prays for the safety of Ellen and John, requesting their concealment remain a secret. He'll pick them up at his next stop, near a town whose name he'll never utter.

Red is relieved to have finally reached the narrow road leading to his aunt's property. Trudging over a large rock in the road, he stumbles. Noise from not far inside the trees lining the road causes Red to grab the musket strapped to his shoulder. Just as he's about to raise the gun to his eye, he sees a frightened deer bolting from a patch of grass where it was eating. He's thankful that's all it is. He tosses his head, laughs to himself and carries on his way. Before he sees his aunt's house, he smells the smoke of burning peat from her hearth's chimney. Passing his dead uncle's old hay wagon, he traces his hand over the worn wooden sides. He wishes his uncle was here to greet him. With no time for reminiscing, he walks up to the front door of the house and enters.

"Aunt Mah-ree?" Red says, giving the door a little tap to announce his arrival.

"Ah, if 'tisn't the piobar, himself," Aunt Máire greets Red, as he enters her kitchen.

"Too bad I'm not 'llowed t' pipe a chune in public," Red says, half-laughing. "'Fraid I'd be hung."

"*Feer in yeh* (the truth)," she says, looking past him to the doorway, making sure no unexpected person is there. "Come in, nephew. Sit down. *C'ead Mile Failte.*"

"I've me doubts I'll get a hun'red t'ousand welcomes where I'm goin'," he laughs. "T'anks."

Aunt Máire is the only living sibling of Red's Da. She motions for Red to sit at her small table while she finishes sweeping loose dirt from the surface of the hard-packed mud floor towards the open door.

Red enjoys two cups of tea and a few biscuits. It isn't hard to miss his uncle here in this kitchen. The old woman's husband is long dead. He was a victim of interference with British soldiers. So she was told. He was maimed during the same battle in which Red's

Da perished. They hung Red's uncle directly afterwards.

"Ya still makes the best tay, Aunt Mah-ree," Red compliments the old woman.

She nods with a little smile while throwing pieces of dried cow dung into the dying fire of the hearth. A thin line of blue smoke soon makes its way around the wooden beams of the low ceiling. From a hole in the dirt floor near the hearth, a chick leaves its mother's side. It staggers to where Red is sitting.

"Ah, 'tis lucky ya are t' have made it past an egg," Red titters, picking up the chick and stroking its little, yellow head with his big fingers.

"*Tá cuma thuirseach ort*," Aunt Máire says, worried her nephew is overdoing it, travelling so far without proper rest.

"'*Tá tuirse orm*," he says. "Tired, indeed, but I'm only payin' me respects before headin' 'cross country. *Aistear anama*, ya know."

"Soul journey, indeed," Aunt Máire answers. "*Cluinim go*," she says, telling him she understands his need to lend a hand to whatever the willing and able-bodied Catholics of Ireland are planning next.

Aunt Máire's old stable houses Red's horse, Bolg. It's a joyous reunion between man and beast. While loosening the rope tethering it to a post outside its stall, Red sings the stallion a song. The same tune he always chooses before the pair travel. To Red's mind, the song is reassurance everything will be alright and there'll be many more returns to this stable, Aunt Máire's, Galway and Inis Meáin. And one day with Ellen and John. Horse and all. Back on the island. Safe from but a couple of the King's soldiers, where they might manage to live in comparative harmony.

Red named his horse *Bolg* (Bul-ug), after a race of people

known as the Fir Bolg once inhabiting ancient Ireland. Their predecessors, the Muintir Nemid, had settled in Ireland and then abandoned it to live in other parts of Europe. Those who settled in Greece became the Fir Bolg. They returned to an uninhabited Ireland and thrived there until they were overthrown by the invading Tuatha Dé Danaan, another group descended from the Muintir Nemid. Red's horse is strong and stubborn, powerful and brave - the same notions Red Houlihan often holds of himself. The name, Houlihan, after all, is characteristic of those boastful or conceited. Together, Red and Bolg are guaranteed to do what has to be done.

Red gives Aunt Máire a hug and a kiss on the face before leaving.

"*Go dté tú slán* (Safe journey)" she whispers.

"Bless you," he whispers in return.

Red has always longed for that day to come. When he and his little family can live out on Inis Meáin. Have more children. Watch them grow. Teach them how to survive the land and this life of uncertainty. But in his heart, he knows otherwise. It will never happen. Unless things change drastically in Ireland. And, sadly for them, life for most Irish in Ireland has only gotten worse as the English continually concoct new ways and means of dampening their spirits.

In 1767, and again last year, in 1777, the English government concocted and instated the Whiteboy Acts - laws strictly defining and prohibiting the illegal assembly of Irishmen. The Irish, determined to put an end to their lives as slaves to land once their own and to a regime of foreigners few will come to regard as acquaintances, pay little notice to the never-ending directory of acts and decrees invented and shaped at will by the English. Equally punishable by the alien establishment is the administration of oaths deemed unlawful.

This amounts to all things Irish in the minds of those representing Britain in Ireland. The posting of notices threatening foreign landlords occupying land and premises formerly property of Irish-born families is also forbidden; even though many landlords are considered absentees, only visiting their unjustly-acquired properties once or twice a year. If ever.

Red, like his father before him, is guilty of all of the above. And more. For what the authorities call *Whiteboyism*, participants of illegal activities are habitually hung right away. Without question. In front of their wives and children. As if to teach them a lesson. Despite this atrocity, many still believe the determination to rid Ireland of the English is likely to remain incessantly powerful. That one day it will result in triumph. Catholics accept punishment as God's will. They'd never dream of steering from the conviction that they might deserve a morsel of serenity. For once in their ragged lives they might experience the often-spoke-of, but scarcely-felt notion of peace. What sensation amity might present remains a mystery.

For neither fuel nor timber are the Irish allowed to cut a tree in Ireland. Not for the construction of homes, barns, or fences. Nothing. Instead, they must rely on peat - the remains of ancient trees fell into Ireland's great bogs, on its way to becoming coal - for fuel. It can often be seen piled in great mounds to dry. The smell of burning peat is heavenly to Irish families lucky enough to be able to pay the exuberant taxes set upon them by those insufferable landlords. *Strangers designated to be their incontestable rulers*, Red's father always said of them. The staple diet of the Irish, potatoes, comes from setting seeds and tilling the soil in all matters of weather. Then the long wait. The grain and meat they produce is taken by the English against rents owed for their humble cottages. What the Irish know of the world just outside their crumbling homes of rock, muck and straw is savage and, for that alone, the plain smell of peat burning is sometimes sufficient to re-fuel their often-discouraged hearts.

The minimal presence of English soldiers on Inis Meáin is of little threat to the island's inhabitants. Local girls there have no trouble seducing young Englishmen. Keeping them company. Especially when local men and boys make plans to raid their barracks for weaponry or food. While food is eaten in a hurry, leaving no trace, guns, bullets and bayonets are hid in the many grikes of the island's great slabs of rock the locals call *clints*.

If beautiful young women aren't enough to dull the soldiers' concentration while watching their posts, gallons of poteen left unannounced at their doorstep prove hard to resist. Especially for lonely young men far from home. The soldiers spend most of their time drunk and, as a result, often lean toward their good traits while interacting with locals. That can change, though, when they know an official of their government is due to arrive for inspection. Updates on the behaviour of locals, ensuring they make good on their tithe payments to the Church of England and are not killing and eating their own cattle for food are expected and given. Occasionally, homes are toppled. Even burnt. If visiting officers feel there might be a bit of shelter beneath the fallen center beam once holding skillfully, patiently-woven roofs, they'll do their best to have their escorting soldiers destroy the remainder with the aid of strong rope and an able horse.

The best an evicted family member can do is screech and bawl. Wallow in pity. Little has changed in the past six-hundred years. Some women, believers in superstition, curse in their native tongue - casting spells upon the British. When the man of a tumbled home threatens soldiers, he's lucky if he only receives a crack in the skull from the butt of a musket. Infrequently, they're shot. Killed outright. Another lesson for the people of Ireland to keep their mouths shut. Follow orders.

With Bolg beneath him again, Red feels a rush of fresh vigor. A few days ago, Aunt Máire had word sent by a relative heading in the direction of where Ellen and John are staying that Red would be by on Bolg to pick them up. It wouldn't be a long visit, but better than nothing. Ellen and John would be brought to another place of hiding, to stay with the family of a Rebel counterpart of Red's until further notice. He'd retrieve them again on his return from the meeting in Cavan. Less than two hours after leaving Aunt Máire's, Red and Bolg arrive at the agreed-upon destination.

Upon hearing a voice mimicking a certain songbird, Ellen and John run from the shelter of trees where they've been hiding. The bird finishes one tune and begins another. A hymn from long ago. One they haven't heard in years. Not since their grandparents' generation dared to sing quietly in their homes, long after their churches were burnt. It was safe to give praise to God when the British weren't around. The rhythmic accompaniment of the familiar dance of Bolg's hooves pounding the earth relieves Ellen's and John's stresses of waiting, wondering and worrying. The tightness of their faces loosens a little. John shouts for joy.

"Shhhhhhhh!" Ellen sounds, slapping the boy across the back of the head. "For Jaysus' sake, what are ya tryin' t' do, have us kilt?"

Paying little mind to his mother, the little boy still manages to jump up and down with excitement. Ellen holds onto his head. Her big hand covering his little mouth.

"*Is binn béal ina thost*," she scorns, giving her son another quick flick of her open hand across the side of his head.

She removes her other hand from over his mouth.

"Sorry, Mammy," he says.

"'Tis okay, John," she tells her son.

"A silent mouth is sweet, indeed," Red says with a little chuckle, reiterating Ellen's words. "Now, c'mon," he says in a lower voice. "We've got t' get on the auld path t' the long meadow 'fore dark."

Ellen wraps her long arms around her husband's neck. One of her hands fights its way through his thick head of tight red curls. She kisses his neck.

"Ah, Ned Houlihan," she whispers, "yer lovely as ever."

Ellen and Aunt Máire are the only ones who call Red by a version of his birth name.

"*Tá mo chroí istigh ionat.*" Ellen's breath is hot and sweet in Red's ear.

"My heart is within you, too, *a stór* (my darling)." he whispers back, kissing her softly on the forehead.

"An' *my* dear, you'll always be, too," she whispers.

She kisses his ear lobe and neck before resting her head on his broad shoulder.

Young John presses his face against his parents' thighs. Both his arms are wrapped tightly around their legs. The three stand in a huddle, enjoying a rare moment's peace. John doesn't weep as he'd like. Big boys of five years don't cry. But his eyes water, glistening from the powerful feeling of being a family again. Love for one another. Something no one can take from you. The feeling of togetherness won't last long, he knows. It rarely does. *Expectations are for the foolish*, John has heard his father say. Not that the boy really knows what that means. He does a poor job covering his sobs.

"*Mo buachaill stór* (My darling boy)," Red says in a low voice,

"*Tá sé ceart go leor a caoin'.* ('Tis alright t' cry.) Means ye have a heart. An' t' have a heart means yer alive."

"Did ya ever cry, Da?" John asks.

"Ev'ry man cries when he has to, me B'y," Red answers, truthfully, probably for the first time since his father was murdered. "T' cry means ya cares. Imagine yer tears are a river. A river that will lead ya t' makin' t'ings better. T' find answers that might keep ya from havin' t' cry o'er the same t'ings again. Tears are just yer heart overflowin' wit' sadness. If ya didn't cry, John, yer heart might burst an' we wouldn't want that now, would we?"

John shakes his head, offering a little laugh while wiping his eyes. Red fights the sudden urge to have a good cry himself. Instead, he bends over, picks up his boy and whisks him over his head. They spin like the water wheels stealing energy from the wild rivers they long to fish without fear of being caught and persecuted. John's hot tears land on Red's forehead, trickling through his eyebrows and over the bulbous tip of his nose.

"A time o' amity," he confidently tells his little family, "will happen in Ireland. An' for that, I've a plan," he assures them. "But first, other matters need tendin' to before we can live a life o' solitude."

"Oh, Neddy," Ellen cries in a whisper, "Ya said there'd be no more fightin' fer ya. What good are ya to us, dead? Jaysus Christ! God forgive me!"

"'Tis possible," he responds quickly. "Peace in Ireland, an' 'tis goin' t' happen," he promises them again.

They ride off into a land they know well, but have never been able to call their own.

"Jaysus, Ned Houlihan!" Ellen's tone changes from one of lenience to dissuasion. "When've the Irish ever won a war ag'inst England? Tell me!"

"'Tis a different world now, *a stór*," Red tries to convince his wife.

"Don't!" She raises her voice above the volume of rustling leaves.

He turns slightly to hush her, but she'll have no part of it.

"Don't try an' tell me, an' our child," she goes on, "that there's 'nough smart Irishmen t' outwit t'ousands o' those bastards!"

"Ellen, listen," Red has to raise his voice, too.

"Shhhh!" John offers from the front of the horse.

"'Tis okay, me Son," Red says. "Mammy needs t' say what's on her mind."

"Ned!" she begins again. "The few guns ye've bought, stolen an' stored o'er the past few years are prob'ly seized up by now. Useless. An' besides, the English likely have bigger an' better ones, even if ye do have 'nough powder an' shot, an' the guns do work."

"The war in Amerikay, Ellen" Red says, "'tis suckin' the life out o' England an' the English. Other countries are fed up wit' their nonsense, too. Not just us, ya know."

"'Tisn't all that comforting, Ned Houlihan," Ellen says with a little less impatience.

"*This* is our time, Ellen, t' get a bit o' control," Red tries to finish his thoughts. "The crowd in France would just as soon crush the English, same as we'd like to. We're no longer alone, *a stór*."

"*éan*," John says, pointing at a bird flying alongside the path, just above the trees.

"*Fhuiseog*," Red says, noticing the playful lark.

The lone bird, any bird, reminds Red of Aunt Máire. It's a distraction, enough to tell Red and Ellen they should be concentrating on now. On simply being together. They agree it's unfair to argue in the presence of their son. John could certainly use any positivity they're able to muster.

"Isn't it beautiful, John?" Ellen asks.

"'Tis Mammy," the little boy says with excitement. "But how come she's not singin'?"

Ellen says the lark is too busy collecting worms and when her babies have full bellies, she'll sing again. John is happy with that answer.

Forgetting their differences, Ellen hugs her husband tighter. She whispers hints of her desire to see her mother in Roscommon, her homeland. But Ned offers not a word. No time for that. Not now.

DARRELL DUKE

# CHAPTER THREE

## *Innocence Lost*

When he first hears the voices of English soldiers, Bolg grunts. As if he'd understood the ludicrous intentions behind the Penal Laws and countless other concoctions invented to eradicate the Irish from existence. The soldiers' audible expressions are venomous. Spewing insolent laughter in a never-ending ceremony of mockery at everything Irish. Red cups his hand and slaps Bolg on the side of the head. The old horse knows right away to mind his snorting. Ellen covers John's mouth until Bolg's soft trot brings them clear of where the soldiers are resting for the night.

Bolg is an old warhorse. Like his master, the animal wears scars of grazing musket shot, bayonets, knives, and the many jagged rocks he's fallen on and tumbled over while tearing through and outrunning troops of Redcoats. The horse's face, chest, sides and legs consist of lumpy flesh where his hair, not unlike the coarse texture and crimson of Red Houlihan's, covers wounds.

"I'll not use 'im in the next fight," Red says, telling Ellen of his intentions to retire Bolg.

"Ya cares more 'bout that horse than ya do us," she lies in anger.

The idea of her husband continuing what she sees as worthless troubles Ellen immensely. She's seen and heard too much in her short life to give her any cause to think or react otherwise to such notions.

Arrangements have long been made for Bolg, where he'll spend his last years and dying days. One place should Red not return from fighting. Another for when they sail across the ocean to North America. Providing there isn't room enough for Bolg on whichever ship the Houlihans can secure passage. Surely it'll be cheaper than buying a new horse in a foreign land. Regardless of what they charge for Bolg's fare.

Bolg appears highly aware of the shade of red on the uniforms of the English. There's been times he's been halted too fast for his liking to keep out of harm's way. Or kicked harder than usual to speed away. His hearing sensitivity heightened, damaged and maddened by musket blasts. Red says the horse gets furious upon seeing polished coats and shiny buttons. Their attire too clean and foolish for warring as far as any Irishman is concerned. Beneath his torn and patched dungarees, Red swears he feels Bolg's old heart racing at the smell of the enemy.

Worn, once-black leather blinkers keep the sheen of Red's short spear from Bolg's sight. The same steel lance fashioned from the bayonet which bled the life from Red's father. Da. Every bang on the red-hot steel held to the anvil in the old stonewalled forge on Inis Meáin reminded Red of each blow Da laid upon the soldier. A time he'll never forget.

In his young mind, Red is sure victory belonged to the Irish this time. Da had the soldier by the neck. The Savage from Galway Bay - what some called Séamus Houlihan - Red's father. But like Mam said, nothing lasts forever. Red secretly hoped his father would follow his father's way of thinking - that it is better to find a version of peace by focusing on an obsession of no harm to anyone. In Red's Grandfather's case, it was building clocks. But his example had no good effect on his son, Red's father, who remained determined to fight the English out of Ireland. No matter the cost. Death equaled martyrdom. Another hero for old Ireland. A legend whose bravery would be talked about, passed down around hearth fires for the remainder of eternity. So they continued to believe.

Even through the emotional impairment of having witnessed his father's death, at the time Red felt an odd reconciliation with the world. Death. The instrument which handed peace to his troubled father at last. There was nothing monumental about it. No magical scenes accompanied by harps. No angels. At least not that Red could see or hear.

"Most men are savages in the blindness o' youth," Da had said, "but even they are capable o' sheddin' rage in their auld age."

"Da died a savage," Red often told his peers of the great paradox.

Red was barely sixteen when it happened.

Watching his father fight the battle destined to set the devil in the teenager forever, he was a proud son - unsurprised, proud even, of the confidence and fearlessness strong in his Old Man's eyes as he strutted around frightened young Brits. Auld Da, afraid of nothing or no one. Always ready for someone to cross him. Armed for battle with his giant arms and whatever he'd made and carried to give the enemy a good clout. Always ready to silence an Englishman. Or Irish traitor.

An enemy is an enemy, Da discoursed. Determined, he was, to steal back the Ireland once enjoyed. Or at least imagined. Albeit six-hundred years ago or more. Before the English decided it fitting to rob the Gaels of their brilliant tongues naturally greased with fun-loving sauce, poetry and song, and their wives and children of what dignity they'd been able to scrounge, hide and keep. Simple things which might help comprise a serene soul. Inside their heads the invaders would never get. And the often-dependable, indispensable Irish wit would one day find a means to freedom from strife. For at least the generations to follow. That's what Da lived and hoped for.

It was during this particular battle that Red despairingly acknowledged his witnessing of a tinge of fear in his father's eyes. Or maybe it was just plain and simple pain. But it took a gush of blood from his Old Man's mouth, covering his torn singlet, for that fear to find its fruition. The sun's light reflected in the tip of the bayonet poking through Da's back. In seconds his strut was no more. In the fury and din of snorting horses, concoctions of shouts, screams and pleas from either side to live or die, God's blessed sun remained striking on the surrounding hills of green. The sun in a cloudless sky would always remind Red of that atrocious time. That life for others and all things nature carried on seemed beyond cruel to Red. It would have been more befitting for dark clouds to cast shadows upon the battlefield. For rain to drench all below, wash blood from the battered bodies and disturbed ground. But no. The sun kept heat to the situation. Slowed rivers of blood gushing or trickling from defeated men. Heightening the horrid stench of death and of death to come. *What kind of a god would allow this?* Red wondered.

From the bushes where he'd watched his father's sure end, Red scampered and scurried like a frightened cat through the carnage. Pouncing on the Redcoat fighting with Da, he held the soldier to the dusty earth with one hand. With the other, he ripped the musket-grounded bayonet from Da's guts. Auld Da fell backward. Probably dead before he hit the ground. No proper good-byes. No warm hugs nor pats on the back. *Riamh amon leisce ort*, Da always said. Never hesitate. Red gouged the terrified soldier in the side, lifting him off the ground. He didn't look much older than Red, and was certainly no bigger. In any other situation, the sound of the soldier's guts as the shocked body fell to one side would have bothered Red drastically. Instead, it provided energy to finish what he'd started. Faculties clever enough to ensure he'd not be captured. If it wasn't for other soldiers running at him from all sides, Red would've carved up the soldier 'til there was nothing left of him. Instead, he yanked the blade from the man, let him fall away, and turned on the next, closest enemy. For an instant Red knelt beside Da, took his hand and whispered *slán abhaile*. Safe home. Da did blink. So he was alive. He would have heard his son's words. Felt the warmth and strength of his boy's well-wishes. He could return Home to The Lord without worry. His mission on earth was compete. He'd done all he could for his family. It was okay to let go. They'd be together one fine day and there'd be peace once again. Da's hand was still warm. And although he was unable to utter a sound, his eyes were sorrowful, but not without acceptance. Relief, perhaps. God's will. God's way. Peace.

Leaving the battle scene, Red leapt over men. Some his relatives. Others his father's friends whose blood surrounded their failing bodies. Their eyes fixed serenely on something a man not dying couldn't hope to see.

While he can hardly recall all the events thereafter, Red remembers only more blood and jumping into trees for cover. Down a cliff. Lunging off big rocks into tree tops. Tumbling over the hard earth toward the sea. Cutting the center of the palm of his right hand on a sharp rock ledge. As he continued running, blood poured from his right shoulder - a wound for which he's had to compensate since. Especially when taking aim with a gun. A flesh wound. Or so he thought at first. One he'd take care of once back in the safety of home or in the forge on the island.

After a mad dash which seemed to last an eternity, Red made it back to his currach. He tossed the soldier's rifle, blood-stained bayonet and all into the bottom of the canvas boat. Then, like the madman he'd become, he rowed back to the island. Salt water

31

splashed up by the oars stung and washed his wounds. Blazing pain kept him alert. Hungry gulls circled and swarmed above. After reaching a beach, landing the little boat was as difficult as ever. A typically-big wave turned the boat over completely. But it was upon sand. In shallow water. Up to Red's knees, if that. He righted the light craft and dragged it through shoal waters. Frolicking children in searching of mussels hiding beneath the salty sand carried on as if he wasn't there. He hauled the boat across the sand and rocks with his good arm until reaching the cliff. There, he untied a large cast iron hook fastened to a chain hanging from above, a device Da had made. Da was everywhere. Fleeting glimpses of his childhood shrouded Red. Running into the surf behind Da and Da's brothers, Red's uncles, whom he adored. He'd pretend he was like them, big and strong. That he was one of the men beneath the overturned craft, over their heads and then throwing the fishing boat across the waves and against the permanently stout swells of Galway Bay. Then pulling the square oars through the cold water in search of fish. Memories of bloated, drowned bodies of fishermen rolling ashore flooded his mind. Their bodies recognizable only by the unique stitches of a family's sweater. Once while out in a small boat, a young Red cried and pleaded with Da and the other fishermen to hook with a gaff and haul in the body of a drowned fishermen who'd been lost a few days earlier from another crew. But Da said no. That the sea claimed the lives of fishermen for all man had taken from the sea. That's where the sea got its strength, Da said. A drowned body had to come to shore on its own; otherwise, it would be a bad omen to those who took a dead body from the sea.

"Show!" Red shouted to the biggest of the boys playing. "Grab holt that hook!"

The boy quickly left his friends and did what he was told, hooking the dangling cast-iron hook into an iron ring bolted to the boat's stern. Block and tackle secured to the top of the cliff would help raise the boat thirty or forty feet. Out of the reach of thieves or mischievous children. So the sea wouldn't destroy it at high tide. Once he reached his family cottage, he'd find lads strong enough to complete the job. Make the boat safe.

"Stay will ya," Red said sternly to the young man, "'til ya sees the lads up top haul the boat up."

The young man nodded.

In the boat's cuddy, Red tied and tucked a sack containing a jug of fresh water and his knife belt. With the dead soldier's gun strapped to his back, he scaled a jagged path up through wide cracks in the cliffs. This seldom-used route ensured his going undetected by English soldiers on duty. It was about half a mile away from the main beach with paths more inviting to those less familiar with the island's rough, natural features. Once he reached the top, doing his best to keep calm, preserving the scrap of energy he had left, Red crawled, fumbled and jumped. After sixty or more fences of perpendicular stones, he finally reached home. As far as he could tell, he'd made it unnoticed. Red's cousins, pretty girls of fourteen and fifteen and in charge of distracting soldiers, must have been doing a good job. There was no sign of the enemy. Word of the attack on English troops and officers wasn't likely to reach Inis Meáin for at least another day.

Upon entering the low rock wall surrounding his family's home, Red's mother rose from the low seat at her small spinning wheel. Red's clothes were ripped and blood-soaked. No sign of Da. The sight of her husband's gun, as well as the unfamiliar musket told Mrs. Houlihan more than she wanted or needed to know. Instant widowhood. Wasted prayers. At the ghastly introduction to her new status, she yelped and screamed. As neighbours gathered quickly outside the rock wall, Red ordered two young lads to go to the cliff's edge. To use the windlass to haul up the boat. With quick nods and no words, they were gone.

Two thin women lifted the dead weight of Red's mother from the ground. They dragged her kicking and screaming into her home. One of the women was wise to keep her hand over the distraught woman's mouth, lessening the chances of a soldier appearing. Men asked questions, but Red heard only his mother. The sixteen-year-old's eyes had seen too much. A lost, entrenched, hate-filled expression filled his face. Though he'd been born into the life of a Rebel, this moment assured there'd be no turning back. One way or another freedom would be had. Da's death another to avenge. His mother's blaring had as much to do with the lucid, shredded innocence of her son as for the grief of losing her husband. Damaged by the loudness of gunfire, Red's hearing was dimmed. Yet his head pounded from his mother's muffled, yet high-pitched cries.

The loud whispers of curious neighbours got on Red's nerves. He sat to the table, in Da's usual place for tea, rested his elbows on his thighs and fought back the tears causing terrible pressure all around his head. He could still feel the warmth of Da's hand, and the sight of Da's bottom lip curled, like that of a frightened child, haunted every last morsel of Red's being. Memories of his childhood in this humble cottage played over in his mind. Da's gentle ways. His strength and determination to help his fellow Irishmen. The never-ending fight to drive the English out of Ireland was portrayed in the stories he told; at night around the hearth fire, mornings on the strand while picking dried kelp and other dirt from the family's fishing nets, in Da's boat with Red's uncles waiting patiently for a school of herring to run into the nets strung from one currach to another. The tunes from Da's whistle after a long day harvesting potatoes and the stories of old Ireland passed down from Da's own grandfather and great grandfather while they rowed the unpredictable waters of Galway Bay to trade their potatoes in Connemara or to sell their catch near the Spanish Arch in Galway city.

The open door of the tiny home letting summer in reminded Red of Da's enthusiasm after the wet, damp and cold season of winter finally passed and the low wooden door let open once again. With the warm winds arrived the perfumes of budding flowers and plants, the whiffs of fresh catches from the nets of fishermen, the loud, now-somehow-tolerable whispering of women in gossip, children playing away the pent-up energies of months indoors, and the laughs and cries of winter babies carried outdoors for the first time on the hips of able mothers or older sisters. Lovely yellow chicks left their mother hens' sides, making their way to the call of the wind's welcome - their first squinted view of daylight and their terrifying introduction to the dangers of always-hungry gulls and bold, stray cats. All of this and more Red envisioned from Da's place at the small room's table. He closed his eyes again.

Since he was a boy, Red had followed his father to secret meetings. But never did he understand the seriousness and brutality of it all until this latest fight. Until this moment, a world without Da in it wouldn't even make its way into the young man's imagination. An impossibility. Sure, patience wasn't always a part of Da's ways. But that changed as Red grew older, wiser. It was then when Red understood his father's need to handle matters correctly and in a sensible, swift fashion.

The Levellers, the group Da associated himself with, were never truly meant to physically fight soldiers of the British army. But plans changed. The majority, long since fed up with their miserable existence, decided they were well capable of destroying a goodly portion of enemy troops. And, as always, it was a known fact some of the Irish men would never see their homes or families again. The mission of these Irish Catholics, Da's particular cell of Rebels, was to wipe out an entire branch of Britain's army due for assembly at a particular location yesterday for some celebration of their arrogant existence. *Not all Rebels will survive*, Da had told Mam. But Mam had heard this her lifetime and never dreamt Da might be one of those never coming home. But they were old, in their forties and tired of the abuse. Much of their lives had been spent living like rats constantly under foot. Waiting to be trampled every waking moment.

The cowardly English soldiers usually struck at night to evict, rape, torture and murder Irish families. With this knowledge, Red's father and his comrades agreed the British would be off their guard entirely in the middle of the day. And right they'd been. Red noticed at least forty or fifty killed or badly wounded enemies at the battle scene - more than half due there. It had been a success, even if most died doing what they were bred to do. Kill Englishmen. Now they were martyrs. Heroes whose stories would be told for generations. Same as the ones Da told Red and the others since they'd been old enough to listen. Red shook himself from his mind overcrowded with memories and headed out the door. He made no eye contact with the growing, curious crowd and answered none of their questions.

In the forge, Red dropped the bloody bayonet into the large, boiling pot. Painfully, with a knife, he'd gouged a musket ball from beneath the muscle between his neck and right shoulder. Although it was inevitably sore, the scarcity of blood told him no major arteries were damaged. *Someone was lookin' out fer me*, he thought. His own blood from the lead bullet mixed with Da's and that of the soldier's rose to the top of the bubbling liquid. It disappeared just as quickly. The strong odour of iron from the brew of blood filled Red's nose, churning up a new intensity of anger. It wasn't until he lay down in the wee hours of the next morning did physical pain really strike. That would heal. The emotional sting, never.

Forged from the enemy's bloody bayonet, Red fashioned two

smaller lances with spearheads. Secured by a leather strap onto Bolg's saddle, the new weapons had a destiny. They provided young Red Houlihan with all the fury needed to help plan and execute the diminishing of, at least, another Redcoat. While he'd love to walk away from war, leave fate to God, he couldn't. Not now, anyway.

In the days following, Red tried to recover Da's rotting body from the battle ground several times. But soldiers by the score ensured that would never happen. Crawling with maggots and buzzing with flies, Da's muscle mass eventually disintegrated around his skeleton. What was left had been set ablaze with fuel and liquor while drunken enemy soldiers danced badly around Da's and other Irish corpses strewn about the small field. From the cover of thick trees, Red flinchingly witnessed the Englishmen drinking to another victory for the British crown and another heap of wasted lives no longer a threat to England's dream of Ireland without the Irish. Though many English soldiers had died in the battle, the major loss seemed to matter little to the Crown. A high-ranking officer, newly arrived to this particular wilderness station, ordered the flames put out. Red cringed, screaming inside, as soldiers readily urinated on what was left of Da's remains. Red prayed disease would wreak slow deaths upon the smug imbeciles one by one. A patrolling soldier passed just feet alongside Red's place amongst the trees and, although he knew he could have hauled the soldier downward and made away with him quickly, he chose to stay put. Silence. The day would come for retribution. As difficult as using common sense and exercising patience was at the time. It was one of the few times Red had ignored Da's refrain of *Ná bíodh leisce ort*. Never hesitate.

To his grief-stricken mother, Red lied. He told her he'd buried Da. That there was no way to carry the body home without being noticed. That much was certainly true. Had there been a body fit to carry. Red could no longer risk the 10-mile row to the Coral Strand and the hour-long walk to the battle site, especially now that word had reached Inis Meáin. Officers of the British Crown went out of their way to intimidate the island's people. They'd find out who planned the attack, demanding names of the Rebels responsible for the death of the dozens of troops killed or wounded that day. In typical defiance, Red's mother would only answer questions from the English in Irish Gaelic. This infuriated even the most patient of British officers who threatened to burn the Houlihan's cottage if they didn't give the whereabouts of the man of the house. Da was farther up the coast, in a tiny village in Connemara trying to sell or trade the potatoes from this year's generous yield. He'd be back in a week's time, Red kindly fibbed to the officers who said they'd skeptically accept the story for now. But, if possible, they'd be back to make sure he wasn't one of the rotting corpses littering the battle site in the woods just above the Coral Strand.

Again, young Red Houlihan had to exercise extreme patience for the sake of his life and those of his remaining family. He comforted his little sisters, Maire, Eibhlín, Madeleine, Sibeal and Erin, and his little brother, Brendan, much too young to fathom the seriousness of the situation.

Red asked God's forgiveness. He prayed never to have to tell such a lie again. Especially to his mother. But when existing the way captive people are forced to live, nothing is guaranteed. The guilt would remain as heavy as any iron pike he'd fashion and planned to carry for protection the rest of his days.

The weeks following Da's death were filled with nightmares for Red. From a rocky hillside, a brass looking glass taken from a dead soldier's belt on the periphery of the fight scene revealed it all. It was there and then, in that reoccurring dream, that Red felt some sort of acceptance. It was accompanied by a strange, ironic sense of restless calm. If such a state could be attained. The deciding moment he was sure would leave him a Rebel for life. His reveries and sleepless nights until his death would be filled with repetitions and variations of the horrific affair. All equally as atrocious as locking eyes with Da falling to his death. And the knowing he would've lost his own life had he given a single second attempting to save his father's. To briefly hold Da's hand would have to do.

Red always believed his father gave him a final nod of approval before he died. The way Da's eyes widened when they met his son's. He always gave his son a sign of sanction. Even when Red never quite succeeded at whatever life lesson Da might have been attempting to teach him, he was encouraged to be his best. Praise. No matter what. Condemnation. Never. Something good had to come of that. The strength remaining somehow in Da's hand Red would always feel. Same as he would always smell the foul odour emanating from Da's laboured last breaths. How he wanted to take away all the pains his father was sure to be feeling. And the guilt of knowing that wish would remain unfulfilled. Impossible.

When the weeks turned into months following the ordeal, Red found breathing less strenuous. His thoughts clearer. His body stronger. His patience greater. Even the guilt borne of the times he dared to smile again dissipated. Remembering the good times with Da became easier. When words weren't necessary, and silence too much, Da always broke out the whistle. *Music can heal anything*, he'd said. When words hid in weary minds, feelings could be found through musical notes. Pleasing resonances carried across the water on the still air helped free his mind. Just as it is impossible to worry when laughing, when he played music Red watched the world and all its troubles fall into the shadows. Peace once again.

DARRELL DUKE

# CHAPTER FOUR

## *Letter from Newfoundland*

Drenched with imagery of Ireland's complicated, disturbing, and often-brutal past, Red's thoughts have always raced. Even long before Da's death. Just as his father had done, it's no trouble on Red to spend an hour delivering with passion tales of England's cruelty towards Ireland's people and its intolerance of the country's once-diverse culture. Including its staunch devotion to music. As a musician, Red's love of tunes and songs knows no end. And if there was one to be found, a harp would certainly occupy his embrace. But those times have long since passed, when harpists were revered by the aristocracy of Ireland. The princes.

"In the airly 1500s," Red often reminds young men of the civilian brigade he'd been part of since shortly after Da's death, "due to their popularity an' influence amongst Irish princes, harpists were 't'ought a threat t' the English Crown."

Queen Elizabeth had issued a proclamation to Lord Barrymore in Ireland to hang harpists, no matter the part of the small country they resided. Have their instruments made away with. Burned. This particular lunacy on England's part always stood out in Red's mind, adding to a never-ending list of insults and assaults upon his country and its people. His blood boiled when his mind created scenes where soldiers entered his childhood home, taking and breaking his father's hand-carved wooden whistle before throwing it into the hearth always burning.

"I'd like t' see 'em try an' take me whistle," he'd say in an effort to get the young crowd going, as if the enemy was at the door.

"'Tis a wonder they haven't turned ag'inst the pipers, too," Ellen had said, ever fearful Red might be targeted. "Especially when 'tis always a piper who leads the way t' great gatherings in protest. An' I'm sure they wouldn't care if you were a piper *or* a whistle player."

Red's childhood nights around the hearth on Inis Meáin were filled with Da acting out tales of Ireland's past. From Da's whistle came ancient tunes which Da said the English could never take away and destroy.

"They might steal our land, an' burn our churches an' homes," Da would shout in mock victory, "but they'll never steal our minds nor the stories an' music kept inside."

"Never!" his children and wife would counter in unison.

The murdering of harpists and the destruction of their instruments, the queen believed, would lessen the threat of peasant assemblies and uprisings. Help England gain a stronger hold over the country. In the same illogical breath she was thoroughly enjoying Irish dance music performed by her harpist in her London courtyard. Another morsel of duplicity to add to the fueling rigidities between both nations. And as if that wasn't enough, further laws were enacted forbidding the Irish to practice their native language, to own land, become educated or even marry. If any of these new laws were found broken, perpetrators were punished with death.

Seamus Houlihan, Red's father, also made sure the name *Cromwell* was known, despised and why. Oliver Cromwell had been a political and military leader of England. His incredulity in the ways of Roman Catholics and hatred of the Irish in general was no secret. He, personally, thought the Irish little better than savages - ones capable of unimaginable atrocities against Protestants settled in Ireland. Between August 1649 and May 1650, Cromwell's murderous campaign was credited with the demise of multiple thousands of Irish men, women and children.

"A pathological hatred of us he had," Da told his family of Cromwell.

With too much lore to comprehend, Red Houlihan longed for peace. Love, and its capability to override hatred, dawned on Red the moment he first laid eyes on Ellen. Until then, everything he thought, said and did was mechanical - the running, the hiding, the fighting. He hadn't cried for ages. Before Ellen, he carried a hatred born of the obliteration of the man who'd given him life, who'd called him son, who'd carved him his first whistle, taught him the songs of his own youth, showed him the importance of learning, ways to deal with the hard roads of life and how, sometimes, most times, it was better to take those hard roads than waste time skirting real problems, never finding solutions. And willpower - keeping your mouth shut - the absolute weapon against people. Friend or foe.

When Da said the English had driven God from their land and lives, Red had no reason to doubt him. He'd heard and seen enough to know it was true. But Ellen's love, sincerity, and her own stories of strife and survival quickly cast shadows on Da's torment. Gradually, Red's spirit once broken by doubt and mistrust became cleansed. Together, Red and Ellen found love - a thing stronger than hate and its conniving counterpart, retaliation. Together was better than alone. No denying that. And when Ellen's belly grew big with child, they were even surer God had returned. Every minute with baby John proved there was more to this old world than loathing and intolerance. Happiness could, indeed, exist.

Through little fault of their own, Red and Ellen have no clue where peace resides or if, in fact, all the world is a madhouse. But word from a place called Newfoundland, across the Atlantic Ocean, indicates the prospect of goodwill prevailing. The letter came from a peninsular town called Little Placentia. Newfoundland, the friend wrote, is a lovely island almost a straight sail across The Pond from home.

*Although Little Placentia is run by the English*, the letter reads, *people's lives are their own and hard-working people are given their dues. A system of mercantilism exists here where men fish on boats owned by Englishmen. Supplies and food are exchanged for fish caught. Like in Ireland, freshwater lochs the Newfoundlanders called ponds are in great numbers. They are naturally stocked with trout just as tasty as the ones back home. And free for the taking without interference from anyone. Imagine that. The forests are thick with endless timber. And that free, too. No limits. And hare by the score. Extra meat for the long winters. Pelts perfect for the warmest of caps and mitts. Land can be staked at will. As long as you use it for the growing of crops and the raising of animals.*

A letter to a friend of Red's in Galway from a mutual friend who'd lived in the newly-formed United States of America before moving to Newfoundland said much more. But Red has heard enough. His mind is just about made up.

"'Though the place don't appear t' have the educational opportunities offered by the nuns here at home," Red says unbothered. "There's ways 'round that," he promises Ellen.

The Presentation Sisters, a religious establishment of Roman Catholic women, began three years ago, in 1775.

"Just down the coast. In Cork," Red says. "'Tis been said they'll be settin' up schools all o'er Ireland. Wherever they're allowed to, I s'pose."

Ellen's parents, upon learning of Red's plan, are doubtful of Newfoundland being right for their daughter. They're sure more opportunity must exist in the prospering States of North America. But Red says no to that.

"Not wit' the English wagin' war on their own people there," he tells them. "Not a chance."

The letter Red's friend received came from a man who'd lived in and fled from the American colonial city of Boston.

"He says killin' is just as prevalent there as 'tis at home," Red re-reads from the letter. "Maybe even more so. If you'll believe the like o' that."

"... and wherever the English are in the world, for that matter, tormenting the life out of everyone,'" the old friend wrote.

"What they calls us here, *Rebels*," Red says, "are called *Minutemen* in Amerikay. They're ready t' call t' arms ag'inst their sworn enemy in a minute's notice. No different than ourselves, really."

Large ships known by Newfoundlanders as *Yankee banking vessels* travel north to collect small fish for bait plentiful in Newfoundland waters.

"Jumpin' ship there has been successful fer many Irishmen," Red tells Ellen.

Folks from other areas of Ireland have landed there, too. Servants for the English. But they soon become independent. Start their own families, and live on half-decent, private land.

"Not the best fer growin' vegetables, mind ya," Red reads aloud, "but good enough wit' patience an' the right combination o' prayers. We could make do, *a stor.*"

Homes and barns of the already-established Irish in Newfoundland are a fast guarantee of good hiding spots for those after jumping ship.

"*Deserters,* they calls 'em," Red laughs. "Until the English gets sick an' tired o' lookin' fer 'em."

Many Irish have to stoop so low as to change their surnames to avoid scrutiny from English merchants at their shops where lists of deserters' names are frequently posted. The punishment for such a crime is often hanging.

"Still better than tryin' t' survive in Ireland," Red says. "An' besides, in Newfun'land there's no end t' the fish an', as rough as the sea can get, boats are aisier t' make use of."

"Aisier than launchin' an' landin' a boat in the rough waters around Inis Meáin, at least," Ellen adds.

Red had only heard of Newfoundland once before. Three years ago, in 1775, colossal flooding resulted in as many as four-thousand deaths in and around the place. In a hurry, the seas rose thirty feet. Hundreds of small vessels and several large ships had been swamped.

"Mostly in the Bay of Plaisance and another bay named Conception," the letter read.

Because operation maneuvers were about to begin in North Carolina in the War of Independence, in the United States the storm has been named *The Independence Hurricane.* Given Newfoundland's population demographic at the time, most of those lost and drowned at sea there were from England and Ireland. Or descendants of the same. Others had familial ties to Scotland and Wales.

Within months of the ferocious storm, word reached back home to Ireland. It seemed almost everyone knew someone who knew someone lost to the sea during that storm. The waves also made their way onto shore where most families live, work and play. For a long time afterwards, bodies were dragged ashore in fishing nets. Twenty and thirty at a time in places. Several hundred men fishing near their home islands of St. Pierre and Michelon, on Newfoundland's southwest coast, lost their lives.

In the Placentia area and other parts of Newfoundland, all is said to be quiet now - as long as a close watch is kept on sky, wind and wave. Death and drowning go hand-in-hand living with the sea, no matter where in the world. The fact many men meet their doom each year while fishing is a reality unlikely to change. Red and Ellen understand that certainty.

Red hopes to have a forge in Newfoundland someday.

"Surely," he says to Ellen, "there'll always be a need fer a forge."

In the letter from Little Placentia, Red was happy to read there is no end to the demand there for barrels and puncheon tubs. Most necessary supplies come from what is now the island's capital city, St. John's, and the mood of the sea determines when, and if, materials reach ports like Little Placentia. Prior to the departure of the French in Newfoundland, Plaisance (Great Placentia) had been the colony's capital.

"I might do well makin' iron hoops used t' keep wooden staves togedder," Red says. "No doubt they could be made cheaper t' the locals if a proper forge existed in Little Placentia."

"A cooper an' blacksmith t'would be of great benefit t' the place, indeed" Ellen says, proud of her husband's looking ahead for the betterment of their lives.

"An' no tithes t' spake of," Red proclaims with his big, saucy grin, not dwelling on the great flood of three years ago, knowing the like may never happen again. "What more could ya ask fer?"

Newfoundland it will be, as soon as Red sees his next plan through. Guns galore from one of England's old enemies, the French, are due to arrive at secret locations throughout the fall and winter, should the weather be tempered enough for boats to navigate the wild Atlantic Ocean bordering Ireland's west coast.

"The Spanish an' Dutch are ready t' pounce on England, too," Red reminds Ellen. "That will also help Ireland, *a stor*, wit' our struggle fer freedom. With their hands always full, the English have little time these days fer trackin' down Rebels an' deserters in places far away as Newf'undland."

Red feels the timing for his family to head away couldn't be better.

"What o' the savages in that part o' the world?" Ellen's mother asks. "I hears they're an awful tribe."

"The only savages there are the same ones we have t' deal wit' here - Redcoats," Red quickly answers. "The nonsense of the English discoverin' North America is only that, pure nonsense. Newfun'land was home t' t'ousands o' Indians fer hundreds, maybe t'ousands o' years before them self-righteous *amadáns* (idiots) laid claim t' the place. No different than they're still doin' in Africa an' other places 'round the world. The English wipin' out entire tribes. Givin' guns t' one crowd an' none t' the other. Makin' their own dirty work aisier. What's left o' the poor Newfun'land Indians now keeps far away, t' themselves, in the island's wild interior. Too treacherous fer the English t' bother traversin', so I heared."

Over the years, Red has known many friends and acquaintances willing to die for Ireland. And many who have lost their lives for the cause. Countless, poorly-planned attacks on the British have been averted and in their place patience taught. Hard-earned lessons learned from watching fathers, sons, brothers and uncles die. In hindsight, having been a witness to the attack by his father and their clan all those years ago, many other occurrences should have been warded off. Red, nor many, didn't want to see the likes of that again. Slaughter of his people.

These comrades and countless others who'd followed throughout the long years came from Galway, Roscommon, Tipperary, Cavan and Meath. With the odd one from Dublin and Cork. Together, they formed a band of reliance and understanding. That one day they'd outsmart the seemingly endless resource of British soldiers. Crush England's hopes of owning Ireland and ruling its people as a means to help offset its great debts incurred from harassing and plundering much of the rest of the world.

Red and his friends don't care what the British call Irish folks willing to die for Ireland. *Rebels* it is. No foolish notions they will always be together exist. But sovereignty of your own life shouldn't seem so much to expect, either.

The smell of whiskey wafts on the warm air. Red's mouth fills with water. His heart overspills with anguish at the knowing he can't shoot the soldiers dead this instant. Get away with it. A disciplined anger over the patience necessary in waiting for their turn gnaws at Red's nerves. Not so much for revenge. But a means to end the dull lives granted them by their controllers. The dread that he and his family's dream of living peacefully on Inis Meáin may remain a dream brings sadness almost too dense to conceal. To get away they must.

Attempts at revenge had had their day, with Da, his grandfather on his mother's side and great grandfather, and gotten them nowhere.

For the upcoming meeting at Cavan, Red thinks of concise lines to share with his fellow Rebels. He'll try to assure them they're a smarter people now. And when younger members of the group shout things like, *The Gaels o' auld, surely, would limb the British bastards, an' all hands would celebrate freedom in short order*, Red will exercise patience and remind them to save their breath, that myths often hold more might than veracity.

For many these days, a great sense of relief accompanies the knowing things have changed. All Ireland's people must be diligent, watchful and keen around the clock. He'll remind his comrades that this alertness need apply when they're awake *and* during the quieter moments they accept as the closest they'll ever get to sleep. And the search for integrity will remain a great struggle as perpetual fatigue fights to interfere with their every thought.

When he was nineteen, while held captive a short period by the British for involvement in a riot near Ballinasloe, Red witnessed atrocities he'd never tell Ellen. Or anyone. Through the rusty iron bars of a small gaol in Athenry, he and other known trouble-makers watched helplessly as bored English soldiers threw the babies of evicted Irish women into the air; the tiny, malnourished bodies of the babies covering the shiny bayonets of muskets. The sound of the bodies sliding off. Onto mucky ground where horrified mothers fell and prayed for death themselves. Only to be answered with rape. Then followed by kicks to the head and body as they crawled to cradle their bloodied, lifeless infants. Like any helpless observer of great crime, Red tussles with guilt – the core component of his secret Catholic upbringing. Another layer of horror dressing his tortured soul he might do well without.

Red is considered a nuisance by the Crown. He'd been apprehended for fighting off a Redcoat taunting and degrading the young women of Ballinasloe merely enjoying themselves in song and dance. If he hadn't escaped, he wouldn't be feeling the warmth of his son's body sitting in front on him on the back of Bolg. Nor the loving embrace of Ellen's arms around his waist. So much to be thankful for. For granted nothing would ever be taken.

Red's attentiveness has been on high alert since. And although his act of survival separated his family for the sake of their safety, he carries no regret. More violence is always certain. He *will* return from the next uprising, supposing he loses an eye or an arm. And they'll make it to Cobh, and down over its steep hills to the dockside where one of the big ships will take them across the ocean wide.

Now, passing the British soldiers, only the love of Ellen and John keeps Red from attacking this crew off their guard. In their cups, they're more relaxed than they should be. He contemplates cutting cut their throats before they could turn their drunken heads. Emotions such as these are the very ones the British want Ireland's people to feel *and* reveal. But Red won't give them the satisfaction. Not now, anyhow.

# CHAPTER FIVE

## *Rebel*

Red Houlihan is a Rebel; an enemy of the English in Ireland. Since the Normans first arrived in 1171, citizens of Ireland had been rebelling against outside rule. Countless wars have been fought on Irish soil. And although Ireland's past involves much more than struggling with the English, it's the culmination of the events of the past six-hundred years which have remained a constant in the minds of Red and most Irish people. To become a nation all their own is a common goal of most Irish people. To live free of authoritarianism.

Amongst his counterparts, Red has a flare for the dramatic. He uses it to rouse fellow fighters. To entertain, too. This aspect of his personality is reserved for certain occasions. Ellen nor John have ever heard Red speak the way his fellow Rebels have; adamantly blaring the end of British rule here is nigh. There have been times, after fights on his knees in the pouring rain, when Red has roared revenge on his potential capturers. Then, in his native Irish Gaelic tongue, proclaiming eternal retribution while carrying the bodies of dead comrades away from their blankets of blood and ravenous rats and dogs to shallow graves and rushed prayers. None of this Ellen and John will ever witness, should Red continue to have his way. But he's often paranoid; nervous word of his sometimes out-of-control ways will reach Ellen's ears, that she might want no part of him. To Ellen, Ned Houlihan is a polite, fun-loving husband, and a father of the finest kind. *Perhaps it is all I need to know*, she tells herself.

When alone, on the run, Red is a lunatic. He has to be. The

majority of Ireland's population has to be mad, or at least pretend to be. Show no fear. Red spent the entire winter and spring of 1778 moving from one location to another - house to house, stable to stable, root cellar to root cellar, between the Aran Islands, Galway, Connemara, and Shannon. That, alone, most here agree, would make anyone wrathful.

Red, John and Ellen have traveled many miles on Bolg today. Now, in the barn of a friend, the Houlihans rest for the night. On the ground floor Bolg is quiet in a stall while in the loft John sleeps soundly in a bundle of hay. A few feet away, his parents try to relax. Ellen rests her head across Red's lap while he leans against one of the barn's large support beams. He runs one of his large hands gently over his wife's head. Her soft hair is soothing to Red's overcharged senses. He speaks quietly of fellow Irishmen, ones he calls weak. How they've reported seeing him and his fellow Rebels all over the place: Limerick, Cork, and Tipperary. Even as far away as Waterford.

"They try," Red tells Ellen, "fools they are, t' get in the good graces o' the British, t'inkin' life might be asier as traitors."

"Ya needn't take tattlers t' heart, Ned Houlihan," Ellen reminds her husband. "Not everyone has resolve enough t' be quiet, 'specially when they're scared."

Red nods his head lightly in slight agreement.

"Men like that," she goes on, "those who make up lies, do so t' keep soldiers off their backs, an' their wives an' children clear o' bayonets an' bullets, can still be good men."

"They're 'fraid fer their lives," he says.

"'Tis true," Ellen agrees.

Not that being a traitor is always forgivable, but Red knows these poor souls are at total loss as to how to deal with Redcoats.

"They're intimidated," he whispers, "at the sight o' British soldiers struttin' 'round fields an' wood paths, burnin' homes an' destroyin' their meager crops."

"How could ya blame 'em, Ned?"

"I know. I know," he says.

Ellen asks Red about the plans he'd worked on almost every night during the winter and spring of 1778.

"There are road charts," he tells her, "trench maps an' coastal routes fer those workin' the cause from the sea. There are the names o' men I t'ink should work togedder. An' the names o' men I knows have no business bein' in cahoots."

"What o' the list o' women's names?" Ellen asks. What's that fer?"

"Them ones," Red answers, "are ones reliable enough t' distract half-drunken British soldiers while slighter, but still vital matters are seen to."

"I see," Ellen says.

Red removes a fairly large piece of paper from his leather carrying bag and rolls in out on the dusty floor.

"Maps," he says. "Points o' location fer all hands 'meet, an' at which times, fer how long. An' under what circumstances we should abort one set o' plans fer alternate measures."

"'Tis all there," Ellen says, impressed with the amount of work to which her husband has committed himself.

"We have t' win this time, Ellen," Red says with conviction. "Many Rebels are sure t' die."

"Oh, Ned!" Ellen cries.

"Not me," he says confidently. "The bastards haven't caught me yet an' I'll be damned if they ever will."

Ellen knows most Rebels would face the Devil - horns, hoofs and all. And most Irish agree the closest thing they'd ever encounter to the Devil are British soldiers sleeping in their castles and other monolithic safe havens while the likes of Red Houlihan fight with disease-ridden, starving rats in filthy ditches for a place to hide and rest.

"That's 'nough fer now, Ellen," Red says, yawning. "We need t' get ye t' yeer next place o' refuge. Then meself t' Cavan."

At Coote Hill, Cavan, Rebels will meet for a rigorous two-day session of preparations.

"Any longer than that will surely stir up a traitor," Red says.

"Or at least senseless prate leading t' yeer whereabouts," Ellen adds while sitting up.

"The British are paranoid, an' rightfully so," Red tells Ellen, his hands on her shoulders. "Suspicious o' everyone an' everyt'ing, near an' far. We knows their weaknesses, Ellen, an' this, they knows, is known t' the Irish."

Ellen lets out a big sigh. She fears for Red's safety. His life.

Interrogation of Irish natives is commonplace. Men willing to kill and be killed for a chance at freedom for their families must be flawless in their discreetness and merciless in their thinking, planning, and actions. Redcoats sometimes fall to accidents beyond their control, but there are always too many enemies for the under-armed Irish to rid completely.

"We needs t' get away from Ireland, *muh gra* (My Love)," Ellen says quietly. "T'ings will never improve here. John will understand by an' by."

Shortly after sunrise the next morning, Red brings Ellen and John to stay with relatives of Ellen's where they will be safe until the Rebel meeting at Coote Hill is done.

Red holds his family close, kissing them on their heads to reassure life won't always be the way it is now.

"T'won't be long," Red assures his family. "After anudder place o' shelter, an' our meeting t' plan the next attack on the enemy, I'll be right back fer ya an' we'll head south on our dear Bolg. We'll stop from time t' time, ya needn't worry. I've places arranged fer food, water an' rest. 'Tis all taken care of, me darlin's. To Cobh. Then 'cross the ocean. T' Newf'undland. T' freedom."

If the precarious North Atlantic Ocean will be so gracious.

With one of his thumbs, Red wipes tears from little John's eyes and face. He then squeezes Ellen hand and slowly kisses her lips.

"That should keep them beautiful lips warm 'nough 'til I returns," he whispers in his wife's ear.

Ellen does her best to smile, keeping a cheerful visage for John.

Red mounts Bolg and off they ride.

Ellen holds John close, this time doing a poor job of keeping her sobs to herself.

Riding away, Red remembers meeting Ellen for the first time.

It was four years earlier, in 1774, during a stopover in Roscommon. He couldn't stay long, as he was on his way to Meath to meet another group of freedom fighters - to see if minds had flourished with better ideas of how to win back their country. The old guard, including Da, were dead, or too tired to bother trying to make logic of the senselessness into which they'd been born.

Red said he'd be back to see Ellen. Court her. He made no bones about that, and stood true to his word. After a typical all-night *céilí* (party) in her village, they walked hand in hand through areas of little interest to the British. Fond of one another immediately, the young couple tumbled in the soft grass of an uncut field. In each other's eyes stood promise. In their hearts, mutual love would soon reside.

On bended knee before Ellen's father and mother, Red requested permission to marry the girl he felt he could be devoted to forevermore. No hesitation on Ellen's father's part made the blessing all the more special. Ellen had told her parents of Red's caring ways, and of his devotion to help win back Ireland. The former bit of information could have involved any young man keen to court the lovely young woman, but the latter carried weight enough to promptly sway Ellen's father in Red's favour.

Aside from the assured love of a fine woman, Red attained a reliable ally in her father who astutely paid attention to activities of the enemy. Red was shown maps, and given written information pertaining to comings and goings of the British in Roscommon. As well as that of local Rebel groups in the area. Ellen's father knew where Redcoats stayed, alternate places of hiding in times of war for both sides, and a list of local people not to be trusted. *Snitches*, he called them. Spies of the worst kind. More than ready to have their neighbour hung if it meant sparing themselves. This sharing of knowledge created a rare bond between a father and his soon-to-be son-in-law. Ellen's father believed Red Houlihan could and would keep his daughter free from harm.

Red had made his way into not only the lives of Ellen and her family, he became friends with several residents of her village, too. This was how Ireland's freedom could be won, all hands knew. Trust. Red, and the Rebels he associated with, trained hard and long in the poorest of weather, on the roughest of terrain. They were not afraid of Britain, and they were long ready to help put a serious dent in its militia of antagonists.

With the American Revolution about to burst into reality for the natives of Ireland in Ireland, feelings of detriment flourished. The threat affected Ireland's homeland cause in more than one way. The English were recruiting Ireland's young men - forcefully enticing them to board ships to America and fight for England. The extent of the irony had scarcely existed in Ireland and the odd sensations it sparked didn't easily bypass the Irish on either side of the Atlantic. Cutting deeply into the Rebel cause at home, hundreds of Irishmen were rounded up like cattle and stuffed aboard large wooden, cannon-ridden boats, issued the best muskets and pistols the English had to offer, instructed, then trained to use them.

Those who appeared genuinely eager to go were likely no good to the rebellion at home.

"The likes o' them" Red said, "are destined t' collapse under the butts of British muskets t' the face."

Ellen's father agreed.

The sight of hanging trees had weakened a once-strong

resolve to win back their country, forcing some to prattle idiotically of the pointed plans and unremitting efforts of their neighbours.

Others who'd left considered the ride to America a gratis one - free fare to liberty.

"Fer a crowd fond of a good joke," Re laughed, "this might be the best wan we ever knew."

Although it was a mediocre shot at Britannia, the Irish would gladly take it. Once in America, they'd indiscreetly abandon their pledge to fight for England, summon all decent Irish folks to build armies of their own and turn on the Redcoats. Or, better yet, leave the new country altogether in search of quiet havens like Newfoundland - leaving war and carnage to the English. Their most passionate pursuit, it seemed.

Ellen's father and Red had grand discussions into the wee hours of night. An odd sense of satisfaction came from the knowing the English had gotten themselves into such a magnificent bind overseas.

In America, the thirteen colonies had merged to break free from the British Empire to become the United States of America. After rejecting the authority of the Parliament of Great Britain to govern them from abroad without representation, they expelled all so-called royal officials. By 1774, each colony had established a Provincial Congress to govern itself. But on paper they still existed within the British Empire. Without physical representation from the homeland, English men and women long settled in America were pressured into paying taxes back to the mother country. To be governed from afar wouldn't suffice. And to accept that level of nonsense from the ones who had encouraged them to settle America in the first place would have been, many agreed, ethically unwise.

In response to this barrage of what the British deemed insults to the Crown, they sent combat troops to America to re-impose direct rule. Then, in 1775, the armed conflict against the British known as the American Revolutionary War, or the *American War of Independence*, began. The British sent armies to invade. Their powerful navy set up cordons along the coast, cutting off essential supplies. George Washington, the American commander, worked with Congress and the states to build armies to try and defuse the influence of British Loyalists in America. Congress determined the rule of George III of Great Britain was oppressive and criminal. So, there, in the summer of 1776, independence as a new nation was declared.

Now, Red and other Rebels in Ireland work hard to keep their identities secret. To the best of their abilities, they'll remain to protect their families. To say they could protect their entire country would be pushing it, but they'd do their best on their own. There is also fear in Ireland that their country may be invaded by other countries looking for new lands to loot. With the English army disrupted by the war in America, some feel it's not altogether impossible. It would be easy to take advantage of the mess into which the English have themselves.

Red has arrived safely at Coote Hill, Cavan. He tethers Bolg to a post in a barn while exchanging pleasantries with men he hasn't seen in a few months. A young boy brings water and oats to the tired and hungry horse.

Under lantern light, Red reads aloud from the Hibernian Journal newspaper. The article speaks of the response to the possibility of invasion from the French or Spanish while their unfailing assailants, the English, are away.

"In Belfast," Red reads to his fellow Rebels, "over one-hundred-t'ousand men have formed a group called the Irish Volunteers. The Volunteers, taking advantage o' Britain's fixation o' skirmishin' in the American Revolution, managed t' force Westminster into concedin' legislative self-reliance t' the Dublin parliament."

From there, three members of the Belfast 1st Volunteer Company, Theobald Wolfe Tone, James Napper Tandy and Thomas Russell, laid the cornerstone for the establishment of the United Irishmen organization.

A man from Cavan speaks up.

"An' as fer the United States bein' a great place t' settle," he begins, "word from a few fellers from here who're after bein' there speaks o' overcrowded dockyards, wharves an' beaches."

"They're fightin' an' killin' one anudder there," another man interrupts. "over a bit o' space t' tie up a fishin' boat. That's what I hears. Even amongst the Irish themselves."

Surely, the world was big enough a place where land was available without having to interfere with a neighbor, they all agree.

"Word from Irishmen workin' fer American skippers combin' nort'ern waters fer bait in their banking barques," the Cavan man says, "agrees Newf'undland might not be a bad place t' try an' settle."

A few Irishmen who'd settled in Gloucester, Massachusetts, and worked for American sea captains in obtaining bait said Placentia Bay was teeming with fish.

"Endless miles o' empty coastline fer stages an' wharves," Red butts in, "an' beaches o' huge, rounded stones perfectly fit fer the drying o' fish."

"Is that right?" a few of the Rebels ask.

"Yeah," Red says. "An' vast, sheltered harbours fer settin' lobster cages an' meadows satisfactory fer sowin' crops. Sure, yer even 'llowed t' cut wood there."

"Wha? No, b'y!" another man says.

"'Tis true," Red says. "A family'd never run out o' wood fer buildin' an' burnin'. An' besides the mainland, hundreds o' islands, mostly empty o' people, exist, too. Not t' mention no wars t' spake of."

"Sure, what are we at here then?" the Cavan man asks.

Newfoundland seems more alluring all the time.

Just as Thomas Jefferson had done for America, Red Houlihan and thousands of other Rebels search for a means to write and instate a declaration of independence in Ireland. But this isn't going to be an easy feat with England constantly in the face of and on the heels of Ireland's people. Still too close for comfort.

# CHAPTER SIX

## *Losing Ellen*

The tiring meeting of the Rebels at Cavan is done. Red has memorized all discussions and plans discoursed amongst his comrades. He and Bolg have been riding all night; stopping at the edges of rivers and lochs along the way to quench their thirst and to stretch and rest. At half-past four in the morning, the sun's light dresses the tops of treetops while other rays illuminate branches, grasses, moss and rocks of the forest floor.

Red and Bolg arrive at the cottage where Ellen and John have been staying. While few words are exchanged between Red and the residents of the home, Red shakes the man's hand in gratitude of the kindness and helpfulness given. Ellen is relieved at the sight of Red while John is too sleepy to give his full attention to the situation.

Less than an hour later while trotting around an outcropping of rock along the path. Bolg is startled by the sudden appearance of three British soldiers who step suddenly onto the path. Three horses are tethered to nearby trees.

"Whoa!" Red shouts to Bolg, and the horse comes to a halt.

"Early for a family outing, is it not?" one of the soldiers ask.

"Da?" little John says, looking back and up into Red's eyes.

"'Tis alright, me Son," Red assures John.

Ellen's grip is tighter than ever around her husband's waist.

"Good morning, Gentlemen," Red says in his best proper English in an effort to gain a bit of respect from the soldiers.

"Yes, it's a good morning, indeed," one of the soldiers says, stepping towards Bolg. "Where might I ask are you people heading at such an early hour?" he asks.

"Wake," Ellen says without delay.

"Allowing your woman to speak for you, Sir?" the soldier asks Red condescendingly.

The other two soldiers laugh while the one asking the questions grabs one of the rings of Bolg's bit and blinders. Bolg pulls his head back, yanking the soldier with him.

Red offers a fake laugh.

"Da?" John says again, fear evident in his voice this time.

"Yes, sir," Red says, politely. "My wife's uncle has passed an' we're to be there fer his wake as airly as possible this day."

"Just one dead Irishman," the cocky soldier says, "and you're in a hurry to keen over him?"

"Yes, sir," Red answers. "He was a fine man an' his wife is auld an' needs all the comfort she can receive from her family."

"Tell me this, you fine people," the soldier says, "where are you from on this cesspool of an island?"

"Cavan," Red answers quickly.

"Really?" the soldier says. "I don't suppose you're aware of a meeting of Rebels held at Cavan the past couple of days?"

"No, sir," Red says. "We've ourselves to be concerned with

and no time for fighting with your countrymen."

As Red is talking, the other two soldiers join their comrade on the path in front of Bolg. One of the soldiers takes a piece of paper from a leather bag strapped over his shoulder. He unfolds the paper, stares at it, then eyes Red up and down.

"Your name, Sir, if you would," the soldier holding the paper asks Red.

"And the names of your wife and child, also!" another soldier demands.

"Pryor, sir," Red answers quickly. "Seamus Pryor. And this here is me wife, Mary, an' our son, Patrick."

"Seamus?" the soldier holding Bolg's bit and blinders' strap asks.

"Yes, sir," Red is quick to respond.

"How Irish," another soldier mocks. "Seamus, Mary and Patrick. You crowd of imbecilic heathens have a minimal list of names to draw from upon birth, haven't you?"

The third soldier snickers.

"Quiet, you two," orders the first soldier who now identifies himself as a captain of the British Army. "Seamus?" he asks again, studying the paper he's just taken.

"Yes, sir," Red answers.

"It's rather coincidental, the resemblance between you and the drawing we've been given of a wanted Rebel."

"A lot of Irishmen resemble one another, sir," Red replies

with a little, forced laugh.

"*Yeess*," the Englishman drawls out the word. "Inbreeding has such consequences, I suppose."

The other two soldiers start to nervously shift and scuff their boots while gripping their muskets tightly.

"Lower your weapons!" the captain orders his soldiers, and they obey the command.

Bolg snorts while pulling his head back from the captain's grip.

"Da?" John's voice is higher-pitched now.

"What's the matter, son?" the captain asks John. "You've nothing to hide, I'm sure."

The moment the captain turns away from Bolg and walks towards the other soldiers, Red takes a deep breath.

"Touch an' go!" he yells at Bolg, kicking the horse with all his might. "Touch an' go! Hauld on!" he says stoically to Ellen and John.

Without delay, Bolg rises on his mighty flanks and lunges forward towards the three soldiers. Taken off their guard, two fall backward, one to his side, then beneath the mad rush of the horse's powerful legs.

"Da?" John's concern turns into a full cry.

"Hang on, me Son!" Red orders John. "Keep yer grip, Ellen."

"Red!" she screams.

All three on the horse can hear the air being forced from the soldiers beneath Bolg's hooves, as they are caught off their guard and trampled.

Wind from the acceleration of Bolg's mad escape oddly provides momentary relief to John, Red and Ellen. Not far ahead, the path takes a downturn where Red feels he and his family will be safely out of the way of a shot, should the soldiers manage to get one off.

But just moments later, a gunshot is fired. The musket ball flying through the air creates a drone. It's amplified in reverberations from the surrounding hills of rock and sparse wood of the mountains. The loudness of the bang startles Bolg. The old horse lets out a scared shriek and increases its speed.

"Heads down!" Red yells.

But it's too late.

A bullet strikes Ellen. For the rest of his life, Red will compare the sound to the slap of a hand on a back.

Ellen's grip around her husband's chest is fading. She falls against Red's back, managing to drag her head towards his.

"Ride on, Ned Houlihan," she whispers. "Keep goin'. Save our son."

Red turns his head around. Ellen's cheery red lips turn deep blue, then white. Her pallid flesh even paler. The lively green of her eyes descends to dullness. Gray. He hardly recognizes her. His wife. The love of his life. The one who had lugged him from the wretchedness of his once-darkened mind, the initial means he'd found to occasionally escape recurrences of Da's ghastly death.

Blood appears in the corners of Ellen's sun-cracked lips.

Over the compounded thumping of their hearts, Bolg's iron shoes hammering the earth and the wheezing of his flared nostrils, a silence arises. What could only be a measly second, to Red seems an uninterrupted eternity. When that infinity finally passes, he doesn't have to ask his wife how she is. The way she has fallen over him, and the strong grip absent from his waist and chest, screams the worst. Red keeps his mouth closed and makes an extra effort to widen his watering eyes. Through blurred vision, he scans every bit of land in sight for a place where he can tend to his wife's dire need. A riverside. Anywhere. Wash her wound. Make her better. Comfort their son. But it isn't to be. The galloping of horses and the screaming curses of foreign voices in their wake eliminate any chance of them stopping soon.

"Have ya strength enough t' shoot, Ellen?" Red asks in desperation.

Ellen says nothing. Red doesn't ask twice. He shouldn't have asked in the first place.

"Wha's the matter wit' Mammy, Da?" John cries out.

"Keep goin', Ned. Save our son," Ellen whispers again, before allowing herself to fall off the horse.

Red looks back to see Ellen on her side on the ground. He goes to stop Bolg, but her raised hand waving them on encourages him to go against his own common sense. Part of him feels this is only temporary; that Ellen will be fine. Though he is beyond certain the British soldiers will open fire on him for his violence towards them. If he was alone, he'd stand there. Face whatever fate has in store. But he's not alone. John is his only hope of carrying on the Houlihan name.

Missing his mother's hands on him for comfort, John screeches and bawls. For the first time outside the tentative safety of their home, Red allows his son to cry aloud.

"Mam-mee!" the child cries. "Why are we goin', Da? Why are we leavin' Mammy?"

From the hardest kick he's ever gotten in the guts, Bolg bolts at top speed. Red struggles for stamina enough to ride while keeping John on the horse at the same time. Snots fly out of the livid horse's nose, catching Red across the face. He kicks the animal even harder. Red's stomach pains and he buckles over John in anguish, trying hard to keep the tears from completely blurring his sight.

Red plans to tie Bolg to a tree off the path, hide John and creep back along the path. Kill the soldiers one by one. Surely, Ellen is still alive. No doubt being raped and beaten by now. But Red does none of this. He keeps kicking Bolg who would have thrown his riders off two long minutes ago, if he was ever going to at all.

Red knows the likelihood of getting shot, and of his little boy being killed if Red goes against his wife's wishes. But where's the sense in running away when the love of your life is bleeding to death off the side of a path? *Save our son.* The last words heard from the mouth of his beautiful wife. The hardest decision Red has ever had to face is upon him. He has mere seconds to decide whether to become a suicidal, murderous savage. Or a man of peace. Hard-working to afford his child a good education. To live to be an old man whose trauma might, eventually, even into glorious tales to both entertain and educate his grandchildren.

Together, Red and Ellen secretly believe in life beyond the grave. He's sure to encounter her again. He tries to convince himself of that. There's odd comfort in the notion. Swallowing, he prays a quick death for his love. He turns his mind from the prospect of any other fate for her. But how can he stop at that? Yet what choice has he if John is to live? If it were just himself, he'd fight the three of them all at once. Chance dying alongside his wounded wife. But there's Andy Hunt in Newfoundland. A place John might do well for himself. Live without fear of torment and ridicule by the English. Red won't stand to even think John might have to live the same as himself, his father and forefathers. The cycle must be broken if things are to change. And to break that sequence means leaving. The leaving of Ireland. Forever. Ellen would want nothing less for her only child. She must be honoured.

After being trampled by Bolg, Red figures the Redcoats can't be in much shape for a very long chase. In the onslaught of hard rain, the air's mugginess is replaced with coolness. Father and son ride away.

Forty minutes later the rain has stopped. The fading gallops of the British-ridden horses give way to the rising refrains of birds. The far-reaching echoes of gigantic Galway Bay crashing upon and clawing at the shores of Salthill Beach and the Silverstrand in the distance momentarily sooth the senses. Bolg is halted where Red knows a stream runs about ten feet from the left of the path. The gently-running stream grows into an audible, misty waterfall cascading over a limestone cliff to a wide, shallow pool below. The new sun lighting the mist shows a rainbow which disappears behind a large tree. Red and John take a few moments to catch their breath and to take in their surroundings.

Blackberries stand out in great contrast to clusters of white clover. Tall, lone lime trees dwarf the more plentiful alders growing around them. Pale purple blossoms of ling remind Red of Aunt Máire's home; the elongated bell flowers of the plant barely stirring in the light breeze and the lush green stems poking through, giving hope. Any bit of hope is welcomed hurriedly in times as desperate as these.

Sitting cross-legged on the soft ground of the narrow foot path to the stream, John picks bell heather. He twirls the pinkish-purple flower between his thumb and finger before plucking off each of the flower's four petals, letting them fall onto his dungarees. He quietly names each petal for four of his favourite cousins he imagines playing with one another on the island far out in the bay. He tells his father he can hear their voices singing on the wind and how he can't wait to run and play with them again soon.

Bolg can't get enough water into him. He laps and slurps without taking a spell. Red is no better. His cupped hands throw a steady stream of cool, fresh water over his head, onto his face and into his mouth.

"Bring the canteen, John," he orders his son.

John dusts the flower petals from his pants and gets up immediately. He unlatches the canteen from Bolg's saddle and hands it to his father.

"You do it," Red says.

"Okay, Da!" the five-year-old says, proud to help.

John kneels alongside his father and lays the canteen in the stream, its opened top facing the flowing water. He likes the feel of the water flowing over his little hand as he makes sure the canteen doesn't get washed away and over the falls. Something more powerful than themselves enables both these Houlihans to focus on the moment while the torturous, fresh memories of their wife and mother linger beneath their hurting hearts. Red's blood pressure is up and he has a headache to show for it.

As Red is picking up John to place him on Bolg's back, he

pauses.

"What is it, Da?" John asks.

"I t'ought I heared somet'ing. Shhhhh!" Red says while laying John slowly back to the ground.

"I don't hear anyt'ing, Da."

"Come here!"

Red grabs John's little hands and pulls him down to his knees.

"Down!" he orders Bolg to his knees, also, while yanking hard on the horse's leather straps of the blinders and bit.

Bolg obeys his master and does so, as quietly as a six-hundred-pound animal can. He's probably glad for the rest and folds his tired legs beneath his gigantic body. John is intrigued by the size of their horse, rarely having seen Bolg's girth at near-eye level.

Sure enough, trees can be seen moving above the path about three-hundred feet away. Men's voices are heard. Red unhooks his musket from Bolg's saddle.

"Crawl 'cross the stream, John," he orders his son who is frightened once-again. "An' find a good hidin' spot."

"Da?" John questions.

"Go, Son! Go now!" Red snaps at him in a loud whisper while pouring powder and shot into the gun.

John jumps up and hugs his father.

"Go, B'y. Go!" Red yells.

John reluctantly lets go, drops to his knees again and begins crawling towards the stream. Red spies an ancient hawthorne tree, its gangly branches spiraling above the alder-covered ground across the stream.

"John!" Red whispers loudly. "Go t' the biggest tree ya comes to an' stay there. Wait fer me there. I'll be back soon as I can."

"But, Da! What if…" the little boy can't stand the thought of verbalizing his fears.

"If anyt'ing happens t' me, Son, keep headin' that way. An' don't come back t'wards the main path. Keep walkin' 'til the hill starts t' go down again an' stay in the woods alongside the river, out o' sight."

"Da?"

"Do as I say, John," Red orders the frightened child. "Yer a big brave warrior, remember, Son? Look at me, John!"

John reluctantly moves his gaze from the ground and stares into his father's eyes. He closes his own eyes and nods his acknowledgement of his father's words.

"Go t' that big tree, Son." Red whispers loudly. "Sit down an' cover yer ears. Hum yer favourite chune, an' before ya know it I'll be back fer ya. The end o' the rainbow might be there. Hurry now! Go!"

John, his terror returned, bolts across the shallow stream and back to his father's embrace. Red cups John's little round face in his big hands.

"That's a brave b'y, now, John." Red whispers, kissing his son on the forehead beneath his bouncing, strawberry-blonde hair. "Go now, Son. Go! Go on!"

John wipes his tears away with a swipe of his shirt sleeve and turns running back across the stream. On his way, he grabs a handful of bell heather flowers - something to focus on once he reaches the tree. Once into the thick of alders, John stops to look back at his father, but Red and Bolg have left as quickly as that. The little boy continues, doing as he's been told, batting away alder branches as he goes. He makes his own path in the direction of the hawthorn tree.

When he reaches the tree, John notices it has grown out and up through an old rock wall. The branches look strong enough to hold his weight, but he dares not to climb the tree in case the bad men happen to see him from the path. In his mind, he hears one of his favourite tunes and envisions his father playing the whistle to him in the little room of their Inis Meáin home he hardly remembers. *Sceach gheal.* He recalls his mother saying the tree's name in Irish. Ellen loves trees and plant life. She believes if her son could take the time to learn of trees and plants and the seasons of their flowers, he could learn the necessity of having patience. John closes his eyes and takes a deep breath, imagining it is May month and the hawthorn flowers are in bloom. If it were fall or winter, he knows he'd be surrounded by birds feeding on the deep-red haw berries.

John thinks of Aunt Máire and all her nice sayings. "God gave us memory," she once told him, "so we can have roses in December." He always loved that one. This lone tree, John notices, has rocks placed all around its base. His blue eyes, same colour as his mother's, twinkle when he realizes the tree is no ordinary tree. It's a Fairy Tree. *Sidhe.* That's what his mother calls them. She said Fairy Trees are gateways between this world and that of the fairies. He's no longer upset he can't find the rainbow he'd seen just a while ago. John smiles at the excitement in Mammy's story and takes his time examining the lower branches and trunk of the tree, looking for openings where he might spy a fairy or two. He's momentarily disappointed there's no sign of a hole *or* fairy. But he's proud of himself for occupying his time the way his Daddy told him to. Surely, he thinks, if he keeps looking he'll see signs of the wee folk. Or perhaps their entrance to the outer world is someplace underwater, in the stream, or at the bottom of the waterfalls below. Maybe he'd find and capture a leprechaun and be granted three wishes. Da always told him leprechauns hide and live in places just like the hollowed trunk of this old Faeri tree. *Faeri*. It's been a long time since John had seen the proper Irish spelling of the word, often scrawled in hidden places, far from English eyes. Mammy scratched it on a rock for him once. Nowadays, most were afraid to mutter Irish words, let alone write them. Fear of getting caught.

"Hmmm? If I had three wishes, what would they be?" John says quietly.

The first one's easy.

"'T' have Mammy back. Her arms 'round me. Just the same as before, when we were hidin' in the woods waitin' fer Da. When we heared the bird singin', but really 'twas Da singin' the song - the wan he always sings when he comes t' get us."

John's next wish is for Da to get back now because all the thoughts of fairies have him half scared to death. And what if a leprechaun, and they so brazen, did poke his head out through the base of the tree?

"The last wish I'd want t' come true," he says, sobbing, "is for me, Mammy an' Da t' be back on the island, safe from the bad soldiers."

Red's loud voice, no whispering, shakes John from his deep thoughts.

"Son. Ya can come back now," Red sings out.

John hurriedly gets up from the base of the old tree, takes a quick look back to see if he might catch a glimpse of a fairy or leprechaun. He bolts back through he alders towards his father's voice, and dashes madly across the stream and into Red's arms.

"The soldiers, Da?" John says. "Where are they?"

"Wasn't them at all, son," Red laughs, his big voice full of relief. "T'was only a man an' his family out fer a stroll, 'tis all."

Bolg whinnies, as if encouraging the two to hurry up.

"We'd better listen to our master, now," Red laughs.

But John knows there's a seriousness behind his father's words. He asks about his mother again, but Red says let's go, we'll talk of it later.

"The soldiers may well be rested 'nough t' continue searchin' fer us," Red warns John. "We've t' go."

"'Kay, Da."

Red lifts John up on Bolg's back, then slips his left foot into a stirrup on the horse's saddle. He mounts the beast, gives the reins a flick and Bolg turns obediently back onto the path. They head down the rocky trail and once they get to fairly level ground again, Red gives Bolg hard kicks to both sides and the pace is picked up immediately. John holds on tightly to the straps of Bolg's blinkers. He eyes a rock facing in the distance jutting out over trees alongside the path. He invents a game whereby he closes his eyes for the count of ten, then opens them again to see how closely they've come to the rock. He repeats this until they're past the outcropping. Then he looks for another natural subject, continuing his game which helps ease his mind while making the trip back seem faster.

"Bolg is still the fastest horse in all Ireland," Red tells John who smiles, forgetting for an instant his mother is no longer in their midst.

The sun is out. The aroma of wild roses saturating the misty morning air is savoured while newly-hatched flies become bothersome.

"What're ya doin', Da?" John asks, watching Red with an ear to the dirt road.

"Seein' if the soldiers have given up or have only slowed their horses," Red says in a half-whisper. "I believe they've stopped, altogedder."

"Where's Mammy, Da?"

"Come on, John. There's no time, *a Rún* (My boy).

Bolg turns his big head, dropping it in front of John's face. Something in the old horse's eyes tells the little boy everything will be okay. The boy imagines the setting sun darkening the limestone of Inis Meáin. An array of colours scattered over Galway Bay momentarily brings indiscriminate feelings of optimism.

DARRELL DUKE

# CHAPTER SEVEN

## *Revenge*

In a dream that night, Ellen rides up to Red. She's on a different horse, but one as good-looking as Bolg is commanding. She stares at Red from the saddleless, dark stallion. Her lips are lovely and red. Her silky hair flowing over her beige cotton dress. The horse is idle, anxious to leave. Ellen's countenance beckons Red to follow. Then she's horseless. Standing. Pale. Bleeding from the mouth. Misplaced amongst a damp forest of slimy, greenish-black boulders and decaying wood. She's trying to communicate. He wakes drenched in sweat and tears, and sits up, grabbing both sides of his aching head. His stomach is hallow. He has to find Ellen. Pain in his throat sends his face into the cool stream of water to quench the thirst.

Creeping out of the shelter of the big tree where John remains sleeping, Red gets up to leave. He kisses his son on the head, whispering he'll not be alone for long. John remains more asleep than awake. His lips form a smile and he quickly falls into deep sleep again. Daylight has not yet found Ireland's west coast. Red must scope the hills for alternate routes to get to Ellen, then familiarize himself with places from where he'll get retribution - all this before full daylight is able to give away his cover. John knows he's to remain where he is, to stay quiet and wait for two of his older cousins who will soon find him and play the day away elsewhere. Where it's safe.

Daylight arrives quickly. Red has scoped the wooded area above the city. About half past 11 o'clock in the morning, he is reunited with his son. John sees smoke from the chimney of Aunt

Máire's hearth rising from the great thatched roof. The house symbolizes a home away from home for the boy. A place to relax. To play with the steady brood of kittens around the barn. Stroke the tiny, yellow heads of chicks keeping warm near the home fire always burning.

Bits and pieces of the Gaillimh river shimmer amongst the forest of ancient foliage. John loves the way massive limbs of the grand trees catch the sun's glow; their branches, trees themselves, where John and his cousins play. Where even Red sometimes played as a child. In the distance, that magnificent fortress, Inis Meáin. It beckons. Afraid of no one or nothing. As metaphorical as the magnified character of Great, Great, Great Grandfather Ó hUallacháin from Red's stories - the island's steep walls of limestone knocking back with ease the bold Atlantic Ocean, yet always ready to welcome brave lads like John back home. Back to his great uncle who loves to sing and dance and tell stories and write. John fancies words so much, his mother always said he'd make a wonderful teacher someday. Maybe even write a book. And wouldn't that be something?

Red and John arrive at Aunt Máire's. Red has no time to waste. He must leave immediately. He puts his big hands on his son's little shoulders and looks him in the eye.

"I won't be long, John," Red says and looks to Aunt Máire. "Pray I find Ellen an' get her back safely."

John begins crying and looks around. Aunt Máire motions for him to come to her at her chair. She holds out her arms. John lowers his head and falls into the old woman's gentle embrace.

"Such a grand boy fer five years o' age, ya are," she tells John, stroking his curly hair. "T'wasn't all that long ago yer Da seemed yer size. I don't s'pose you'd like a sweet biscuit?"

John looks up at his Great Aunt and smiles.

"Show," Aunt Máire says while moving John to one side.

She gets up and goes to her kitchen shelf and reaches for a plate of biscuits.

"Freshly baked just fer ya, me B'y," the old woman says with a smile, setting the clay dish on the worn, wooden table.

Aunt Máire sits back in her chair and motions for John to sit in the other chair at the table. She reaches down and picks up a ceramic jug.

"A sweet biscuit's no good wit'out fresh goat's milk," she says, pouring the white liquid into a mug.

"Whatta ya say, John?" Red asks his son.

"T'anks," John says.

"Anyt'ing fer me two favourite b'ys," she says with a big smile.

"Alright," Red says. "Time fer me t' go. You'll be best off playin' wit' the chickens in yer secret place in the barn, John."

"'Kay, Da," John says.

"I'll be sure an' take 'im up t' the barn soon's he's done his biscuits an' milk," Aunt Máire assures Red, knowing John's better off concealed in the hidden space beneath the barn until Red returns, should British soldiers appear.

"Brendan was by, Neddy," Aunt Máire says, seemingly reluctant to tell Red of his brother's visit, especially understanding Red's need to leave and find Ellen.

Red tenses, knowing Brendan is in with a crowd of radicals daft enough to muddle even the finest of plans.

"Jaysus!" Red says, cupping his forehead in his hand. "It's been ages since I laid eyes on 'im. Where's he to?"

"He wouldn't say," Aunt Máire answers. "Only t'was time t' take back what was theirs. An' ya knows what happened last time we heared that! He was away wit' the fairies, if ya asked me."

"Ah, Jaysus! We'll never see 'im again," Red sighs in anger.

He closes his eyes for a moment and shakes his head, then gives his aunt a quick hug.

"Don't forget t' pray fer Ellen."

"Ya needn't worry 'bout that," she says, patting him on the arm. "Remember, Neddy. *Riamh amon leisce ort.*"

Red's eyes water. Memories of Da fill his mind.

"I know," he whispers, "Never hesitate."

With a quick nod, he's gone.

With John tucked safely away, Red takes Bolg to the stable of a friend. He then heads back to the hills to find Ellen.

Red runs through the woods, ducking branches, crawling through rabbit paths, hopping rock to rock across rivers and under falls. When he gets around a prominence facing, he's at a point where he's able to determine, roughly, where Ellen is. He hopes the soldiers will be near, too.

Red climbs a steep bank of grass and exposed tree roots. When he reaches the top, he walks, bent over, to help keep his cover.

He drops to his knees alongside a stream, stretches out both arms and thrusts his head toward the quivering, cold, moving water. In the stream's reflection warped clouds drift. Red notices new lines around his eyes and on his forehead, as he laps at the water like an old, dying dog.

The emotional turmoil of the past twenty-four hours' maddening events have caught up to Red. In tall grass he rolls onto his back with the intention of closing his eyes for a few moments. Instead, he falls fast asleep. Again, Ellen appears in his dream.

In dense woods, she is ahead of him. Scornfully, she demands him to find her. For his leaving, she's furious. 'But ya said, *Go!*', he shouts, although he cannot see her. 'Ya said, *Go on! Save our child.* An' he's safe, Ellen. He truly is. He's at....' Thunderous squawks from giant birds swooping madly overtop primeval trees startle Red, interrupting his thoughts and words. Finally, he catches a glimpse of Ellen. She's on her knees, leaning into the trunk of a giant oak, sobbing. Not far away is a massive wolf, sure to make a meal out of her if Red doesn't act at once. Red reaches her, and the moment he lays his hand on her shoulder, she flies away; the swooshing of her large wings through the cooling air sends chills up his spine. Her red hair, caught on the wind of accelerating flight, flows behind her feathered back. Her feet are pitch forks. Guiltily, Red is glad she's heading in the opposite direction. Her great wings smash through thick branches, sending hardwood limbs soaring like spears toward him. He scrambles for shelter behind a tree, then trips, falling into a stream. Sharp rocks pierce his forearm and blood flows rapidly past his elbow, around his bicep and just below his injured shoulder. He tries to get up. "Red," he hears again. Ellen is back, and by the same tree from where she took flight just moments earlier. This time, she's facing him. "Get up," she says. "Ya have t' get up an' fight fer Ireland. Save our child, Ned Houlihan! Save our boy! Go t' Newfun'land, Ned! Ye'll be safe there." "But Ellen, wait," Red cries.

"I'm here t' take ya home. I'll soon be there. I'll be there soon, *muh gra* (My Love)."

He runs. But each step gets him nowhere. The wolf reappears from behind a tree. It's wearing a red coat with shiny brass buttons. It smirks, showing its teeth dripping with blood. Red makes for the wolf, but trips in a large root, twisting his ankle. He falls. When he looks up, the wolf is gone. So is Ellen. Giant birds swoop above the trees again, their shadows turning day into night. Red caresses his bleeding arm. Then he awakes.

The stream's water is rushing over his protruding arm supporting his head. He hears a faint scream.

"Ellen!" Red says, then hushes himself suddenly, afraid he's given away his presence.

Jumping up, musket to his eye, knees slightly bent, Red turns full circle. Although he sees no one, he determines he's closer to the path than he'd first thought. One of his boots kick loose rocks at the river's edge.

"Houlihan! You rebellious fool! Come get what's left of your precious wife!" an angry English voice shouts.

Red *has* been heard. But he also thinks it coincidental, the timing, the soldier shouting out just to see if Red is near. Regardless, he has no intentions of letting them know he's this close. But his reputation has taught the enemy otherwise. Still, he has to stay put. Make them believe he's headed back to Inis Meáin where they wouldn't suspect he'd go, given the presence of soldiers there - going to where they are might mean certain death and worse, the possibility of them finding little John. Red says a quick prayer for the safety of his mother, family and friends on the island. Still, due to the lack of soldiers in Ireland as a whole because of the American Revolution, he's certain that word of Ellen's plight has yet to reach Inis Meáin. But that won't take long, the way people love to talk.

Now, with the soldiers' paranoia, the tension here in the hills intensifies. Since Aunt Máire had paid her dues with the life of her husband, the Brits, for some reason, avoid her and her land. Perhaps it has to do with the fact she swore on them in Irish, saying they'd pay for their evil ways. Irish lore holds grand might and more than one soldier of England has lost his mind swearing on encounters with the ghosts of men, women and children they've knowingly killed without just cause.

Red smacks biting flies from his forehead and neck. He quickly wipes blood from his fingers onto the leg of his pants, as he pushes one foot in front of the other through the thick trees. He trips in an old stump, falls forward, driving a hard, dead tree limb into the side of his face. He lands on his side, fighting the urge to swear. He rubs away some of the pain in his face with his hand. He looks at his hand to see how much blood he has lost, but there is none to be seen. He's certain the noise from the dry limbs of the forest floor as he fell has given him away. He waits, but hears no indication to justify his fear. He gets up on one knee and uses his hands to push himself back to his feet. Tilting his head back, he then turns his neck slowly from side to side to get his bearings again. He continues walking towards the path.

When he's close enough, Red peers through alders to the path where four soldiers stand; each pair about a hundred feet distant from the other. Two face down the hill, the others up. No sign of Ellen causes Red to believe there is, at least, one other soldier keeping his hand over her mouth. *How could she be alive yet?*, he wonders. They must have administered care to her wound, no doubt as a means to capture Red. It is not unheard of for soldiers to keep beautiful Irish women alive for the purpose of shipping them back to

England as wives or as slaves to higher-ups in the King's army, either. Whatever their reason for leaving life in her body, Red is relieved. He must save her. Now.

To avoid them determining the direction from which he might attack, Red inches backwards about twenty feet and begins crawling downwards. After fifteen minutes or so, he stops, stooping to see where he is in relation to the soldiers. He is only about ten or twelve feet from the main path, he concludes, and about seventy feet below the soldiers facing down the hill. From his pockets, Red draws palm-sized rocks. He has to act quickly to execute this, his only plan for the time-being. He figures the front soldiers have walked down the hill far enough where the back ones can no longer see them due to a precipice of rock where the path winds ten or fifteen feet. They are more nervous than ever, proving so by breaking their line of sight with one another. This flaw, Red will use to his advantage. Time to be extra vigilant and merciless. In his head, Da's voice shouts, "*Riamh amon leisce ort!* Never hesitate!"

Red left his musket behind, at the base of a tree, for a gunshot blast would give him away. Surely then, Ellen would be finished.

Red throws the first rock uphill, in the direction from which he's just crawled. The soldier on Red's side of the path turns immediately. He raises his musket, pointing it above the alders and towards the thick woods.

"What is it?' asks the soldier on the other side of the path.

The soldier on Red's side says nothing, only motions his head for his partner to join him. When they are standing alongside one another, Red throws another rock farther up the hill on the same side, hitting an old, dead tree. It falls through brittle branches and off the half-rotten, hollowed trunk. The young soldiers panic, wasting their single-ball shots aimlessly into the woods. Red uses these few seconds to crouch and dart across the path, into thicker, lower brush. His dark-red head of hair and green shirt give him some cover amongst the ferns and other foliage.

Red thinks he hears Ellen again, then questions the sound. Her voice hasn't left his mind since she was shot. He questions his sanity. It wouldn't be the first time he'd heard a voice that wasn't there. But he cannot give up hope. He still feels Ellen's clammy grip around his body before she fell off Bolg.

The back soldiers must be making their way down towards the commotion because the now-frightened Brits in front, fumbling to reload their weapons, are waving their muskets every which way shouting, "Stay back! Stay where you are! They're on this side, likely headed your way!"

Red's plan worked; they think he's with company. He has them back-on. Time to act. From his belted case of hand-made knives, he hauls out two of the heaviest. Grabbing an end of one, he stands, drawing back his big, well-trained left arm. With a quick prayer, he throws the knife up the hill, across the path. The soldier closest to Red lets out a sudden huff, dropping his musket. The steel bayonet of the soldier's gun catches on a tree branch. The weapon stands on a forty-five degree angle, its wooden butt resting on the ground. Blood spurts from the wounded soldier's mouth, over his chin and neck and down across the neatly-fastened brass buttons of his uniform.

Between the time Red throws the first knife and when the wounded soldier reaches around to grab the blade in his back, Red scurries low, not unlike the rats he's shared ditches and caves with much of his adult life. Another five or six feet gives him better aim at the second soldier. Da had taught him a valuable lesson in killing the enemy - never put a handle on your knives, make them one continuous blade, sharp from one end to the other. Supposing the knives hit their target sideways, they'll still bring harm. When the wounded soldier reaches for the knife in his lower back, he slices his shaking hand. He sounds a mournful yelp. Holding his bloodied hand in front of his face now wet with tears, the soldier's expression radiates terror and disbelief. The blade remains in his spine, the rapid loss of blood draining life from his body. This distraction allows Red time to stand and prepare for the next assault while the second soldier pays attention to the wounded man. With a piece of leather to protect his throwing hand, Red carefully removes another blade from the belt.

The instant the unharmed soldier stands straight to take aim in whatever direction he supposes the Rebel is, Red lets go the blade. The moment it leaves his fingers, he fears he's made a critical mistake. The newest deadly blow might well give away his direction to the other two soldiers surely making their way towards the commotion. Now he wishes he hadn't left his gun behind.

The second soldier falls to his knees, grasping his neck spurting blood like a fountain. Red races onto the path and up the hill. The soldiers are injured, dying quickly. The first one he'd hit is laying face-down in the grass, stirring, moaning, but of no threat. The blade remains lodged in his lower, middle back. Red reaches to the ground and grabs the musket of the solider still grasping his own neck. Suddenly, Red is in the grip of the soldier's bloody hands. Red effortlessly shoves the man away, letting him fall on his back where the soldier, again, places his hands around his neck now spewing a stream of blood. His gaze begs for mercy.

Red recognizes him as one of the three soldiers Bolg ran down, and wonders if it was this soldier who'd shot Ellen. For the sake of concentration, Red fights off the rage. His first thought is to shoot him, put him out of his misery, but a gun blast will surely rob precious seconds away from his next plan of action. Instead, he pounds the enemy's head with the butt of the soldier's own ten-pound musket. Not another sound is heard from him. Red then reaches into the man's carrying case and coat for musket balls and shot. From the keg he'd ripped from the soldier's belt, Red pours powder into the musket's barrel, then drops a lead ball in after it. He dislodges the ramrod from the side of the gun, inserting it into the barrel. When the lead ball is shoved in as far as the powder, he adds a little more powder, then a small load of shot - a concoction guaranteed to do great damage. His hands are shaking, as he fumbles with the ramrod, to put it back in its place. But, instead, to save dear moments, he lets it fall to the ground. As the first victim isn't loud enough to pose immediate threat, Red mumbles a quick prayer for the dying man, asking God for His forgiveness, and decides to leave the man be. He grabs the other seven-foot-long musket still dangling against the tree and begins moving forward, up the hill. He stops and turns.

"*Tá brón orm* (I am sorry)," Red says, having been told a lifetime that forgiveness might lead to some sort of contentment.

He makes the sign of the cross towards the suffering soldier and continues up the path.

"Ned!"

It's Ellen. Her voice is forced and strained, telling of much agony.

Red crawls on his stomach, his elbows and knees moving him slowly over the rocky path. A loaded musket fills each of his hands. Footsteps are coming his way. Closer. Closer. He hears Ellen's muffled moans. She must be on a stretcher or soldier's back, the way her breath pushes forth. Red raises his head for a better look. He's about twenty-five feet away. Ellen is draped over the back of one of two visible soldiers. Red regains his energy, tumbling, diving and rolling into the bushes. The moment the Redcoats see him, Ellen is dropped like a sack of potatoes to the hard ground. No sound is heard from her. A soldier fires. Then the other. Red's upper left leg goes cold, then scalding hot, not unlike the cruel sensation of molten steel splashing on his skin in the forge. He's been shot.

Keeping their distance, the soldiers shout they'll let his wife go in exchange for himself. Red says nothing. Ellen says nothing. He knows little life, in any, remains in poor Ellen, but what's the best thing to do? He'd sooner die than live with the guilt of putting her in such a troubling state and not saving her. He should have listened to her ages ago. But it's too late. He decides he'll go out shooting. But he can't well leave John to his own devices at five years of age. After what has just transpired, surely the army will kill Aunt Máire, John, and anyone else associated with Red. He must kill all the soldiers and hide their bodies, so word doesn't reach their commanding posts anytime soon. He, Ellen and John will have time through the night to make it to a leaving ship. The King's army knows well enough Red Houlihan won't be caught without a bargaining chip, and Ellen's death will surely end their plan. At least for now. Red hopes the soldiers will leave Ellen, so he may return to save her. Or bury her. He can't jeopardize Ellen further by firing a musket ball in her direction. He can't. Should he try? No!

Nightmares of Da's miserable ending flood his mind once again.

# CHAPTER EIGHT

## *Patience*

The soldiers made the decision to retreat and wait for Red and his non-existent companions to make the next move. All night long, Red monitors the soldiers' fire flickering through the trees, not too far from where he last saw them. Now and then, the glow of flames illuminates the material of a soldier's uniform, swelling Red's rage like the tides of the bay. He runs his fingers through his hair, pulling on his curls to keep him awake. Every few seconds he shakes his head to help retain focus.

The events play over and over in Red's mind. When he was shot, instinct said *fire back*. But, for fear of striking Ellen, he remained quiet. Emotionally tortured, though he was, as to whether or not he had made the right decision.

When it seems the soldiers are settled for the night, Red rolls downward, slowly, as quietly as possible. He manages to clumsily hurdle himself over an eight or ten-foot rock facing for protection, should the soldiers attempt sneaking upon him at his original position in the dark. A cluster of stunted trees help break his fall, as he puts all his weight upon his good leg. He expects the soldiers to come closer, but they don't. Maybe the crackling of dry, burning wood has stolen from the noises made by the breaking branches and disturbed trees of Red's fall. Either that or they are afraid they are outnumbered. Either way, Red is relieved for the time being. He lies, his back against a rock, and faces the top of the ridge from where he has jumped. The loaded musket in his grip allows him a slight notion of relative safety. Though new cuts and bruises acquired from the plunge require attention, he won't chance stirring again until darkness long covers the land.

The lack of common, cocky banter between the soldiers, whom he's determined are still just two, speaks volumes of their dread. Still, Red wants to keep going. To save Ellen. Slipping in and out of sleep, he decides crossing the path too risky to attempt, sneaking back to where he left his musket last evening. He also hopes the gun of one of the soldiers he has killed will remain unseen, below the thick ground cover, where he shoved it before jumping over the rock facing. He'll send a trustworthy lad or two back for both muskets another time, when the next inevitable ruckus diverts everyone's attention from this one. It won't take long for word of this fight to get out, he knows.

Now that he's injured, Red knows it's best to get properly seen to, to rest again before continuing his fight to get Ellen back. He and Aunt Máire have devised a plan to help Red make it back through Galway City unnoticed. She'd put together an outfit of women's clothes which Red would wear before hitching an arranged ride at an agreed-upon location not far from where Red is now.

But this is not what Red had in mind - to be leaving Ellen. To resort to the back-up plan is the last thing he wants to do. He would find Ellen, go through any means to rescue her, and carry her home. His heart is breaking at the outcome of his plan. Tears blur his vision and soak his face and beard. Overshadowing the pain from the gunshot wound at times is the lump in his throat. Depression weighs both physically and mentally upon his head. He finds it hard to breathe. Poor Ellen.

Red undoes the three copper buttons keeping the thick leather cover of his blade belt closed, removing a small blade. He cuts off one of his shirt sleeves before dabbing turpentine on his wound, then covers it in moldow from a dead tree. Cloth tied tightly around his leg, just below the knee, will help get him back to Aunt Máire's where hot water and primeval remedies to properly clean and dress the leg may be applied. Then, once rested enough to his liking, he'll leave again to save Ellen. He'll put up with the pain, and anything else he must endure, as long as his wife is back in his arms safely.

Between dark and dawn Red grabs a tree branch to help him stand. Guardedly, he walks beneath the thick refuge of woods, heading south, as if he were leaving Galway City, toward Claire. At the end of the forest line, tucked beneath the fallen wall of an old barn, are the women's clothes and walking stick Aunt Máire promised would be there. Red struggles to get a dress on over his large frame and grabs the walking stick. He tucks two separate garments into the chest of his dress. He ties an orange bandanna over his head of curls and a blue one around his neck in an effort to hide some of his beard. In disguise, he walks as straight as he can to where the end of the rock wall meets the road. While awaiting his ride, he arranges the handful of flowers he has picked along the length of the wall. A horse and wagon soon appears and stops, as Red pretends to be smelling the flowers and enjoying the calm Galway morning.

"Ah! T'was never a finer specimen from Inis Meáin," says the young man handling the reins. "I've seen tidier beards on younger lasses, though. Haul yer scarf more 'round yer face, b'y!"

"Mind yer gob, ya saucy divil," Red snaps, his old woman's voice quivering, not quite where he wants it yet.

No further words are exchanged between the two for the moment, as Red scrambles into the back of the wagon. They head off along a busy road. Passing the quay, looking out under his cream-coloured, woolen shawl, Red sees the hooker he'd rode in on from his island. The urge to catch another ride back home is strong, but leaving is hardly an option. The swans wade and honk, sticking their long necks underwater, as if everything is normal.

"*Folaigh* (hide)," the young driver calmly tells Red.

Red falls back, hauls in his stocking feet, and pulls a dirty sheepskin rug over his body. The driver shoves two small bales of hay he was using as a back rest down on top of Red who curses with fright, but stays still.

"Sit yerself up, auld woman!" the young driver says through the side of his mouth.

"Jaysus, ya just told me t' get down," Red calls back from beneath his cover.

"T'row up in the pail, an' keep yer shawl o'er yer face!" the driver warns in a panicked voice.

Red pretends to vomit, using a high-pitched voice to moan and groan between fake purges and spits, as four armed Redcoats surround the wagon.

"What's the matter with this old battle-axe?" a soldier pompously asks the driver.

"That auld battle-axe, sir, is me grandmudder," answers the young driver, "if ya don't mind, an' I don't know what her matter is, sir! But I wouldn't get too close, sir, if I was you."

The driver begins a hacking fit, and spits on the ground alongside his wagon.

"No disrespect, fine sirs," he apologizes, "but half our family's sick like this. Even the doctor won't come handy t' see us anymore. If ya asked me, there ought t' be a law ag'inst the like 'o that."

"Enough of your natter, you useless specimen of life," the soldier shouts, his nasally voice rising at the end of each phrase. "Keep going, and bring that old thing far into the country, away from the healthy few that are left around this dungeon of a town."

"'Deed I will officers," The driver pretends to obey. "'Deed I will."

Red continues his act of purging and choking until the soldiers are out of earshot.

"Ya can give it up now, Mr. Houlihan," the boy driver says.

"How's yer Da, Michael?" Red asks.

"Ah, not good. Still bawlin' o'er Ma."

"Jaysus, they got her, too?" Red asks.

"Oi!"

"Bastards! Sorry lad. "

"Oi! An' we're terribly sorry 'bout Ms. Ellen, sir."

"Lots t' be sorry fer in Ireland, Son."

"Did ya get 'em back, Mr. Houlihan?"

"Never mind that, Michael. 'Nough o' the questions now. T' Aunt Mah-ree's, Son."

"Oi, sir."

Red was so caught up in character, being an old woman and throwing up in buckets, he'd forgotten about what had happened to poor Ellen - that it was really real, and what he had yet to do to right it all. He knew he was hiding from British soldiers, but had forgotten exactly why - an invention of fleeing all his life. For a while, it was just another day in his mad existence; trying to be invisible to the British - an iota in the collective conscience of Ireland's people. What else was new? Bolg safe at a stable while Red tended to business. It was as though this casual ride through town was normal, the meeting with the Rebels hadn't taken place, and he'd just left his passage alongside the many hookers lining the quay. It seemed mere minutes ago he'd bummed a light and savoured the smoke of his pipe in the shelter of The Arch against the cool, light rain. How he couldn't wait to see Ellen and John after such a long spell apart. The recent meeting with the Rebels would be his last. He'd collect his family, and take passage. To Newfoundland. Start a new life.

Heading back through the large town, people look and act the same as ever. The incessant aura of nervousness always prevalent. They push barrows, plough fields in the distant, call out from shop doorways, shoo cats from flakes and baskets, and whistle their dogs back home from chasing rats to help keep sheep and cattle on track. Red winces from the mounting pain in his leg and, beneath the dress he's wearing, he sees blood oozing through the natural gauze of Old Man's Beard and the shirt-sleeve bandage. Many flies have left rotting fish liver barrels to feast on Red's wounded leg, and he burns his last bit of energy fanning a small piece of flat board to try and shoo them. He soon gives up, too spent to waste further energy, leaving the inevitable maggots to clean the wound better than the soap and water he has yet to access. By the time they reach Aunt Máire's, he is solid. Asleep.

"Never looked so good in a dress me own self," Aunt Máire says, shaking Red's shoulder with her hand, in an attempt to bring a little light to the awful situation.

Red jumps back, reaching around for the gun Michael, the driver, hid beneath the cart.

"Ah, Jaysus, Aunt, ya scared the daylights outta me, girl!" Red laughs, momentarily, again forgetting his predicament; Ellen's miserable fate.

Aunt Máire says nothing, but her concerned expression asks of Ellen. Red gives a quick shake of his head, as if though, once again, he'd forgotten about the events of the past two days and is reminded in a hurry. Tears pour over his cheeks, as his head falls back against the bales of hay. He's embarrassed for the whole thing. Ashamed of himself for losing his wife. The mother of their only child.

"*A Ghrá mo Chroí*" he cries. "My heart's beloved is gone, Aunt Mah-ree. I couldn't get t' her."

Aunt Máire makes the sign of the cross over Red, then over herself before bursting into great sobs. After a minute or so, she quickly regains her customary, sturdy composure.

"Want me t' fetch poor John?" she whispers, making the sign of the cross over her breast again. "T' let 'im know ya haven't found his poor Mudder?"

"Not yet."

Red asks Michael and Aunt Máire to never repeat what he's about to tell them. Otherwise, it wouldn't be long before versions of this information flow from drunken lips into the wrong ears and Red will have little chance of surviving another week.

Wringing her hands, Aunt Máire cringes at the image of the young soldier lying face-down, bleeding and paralyzed, and of the other one trying to hold the blood in his throat to stay alive.

"At least ya had the decency t' give him a quick deat' wit' the butt o' the gun, rather than leave 'im there sufferin'," the old woman says, assuring her nephew he's not nearly as bad as he feels. "Ya did what any decent human bein' would do," she says with a stern shake of her little head, patting Red's good leg.

She pities not Red's wound, but the fact he had no choice but leave his loved one to die in order to save their son. The leg will heal. His heart, never - just as Aunt Máire's heart would never mend over the murder of her husband. Part of her, inside, does a celebratory dance over Red's actions, but she'd never let on.

For not knowing Ellen's true fate, obeying her final wish, Red Houlihan, the most stubborn creature living, so his wife always reminded him, feels tortured. Yet, strangely, there is relief and understanding in the fact he's still alive. Not regret. Remorse, yes. But never regret. He listened to his darling wife in her most urgent time of need. What God intended. If they'd killed Red first, Aunt Máire, too, understands, they'd have killed them all. Now, because of his father's actions, John might have half a chance in life; some sort of peaceful existence, now that his father is alive to help. If Red can keep his head about him, that is. The weight of assuming, and half wishing Ellen's suffering is over, is more than bittersweet.

"Let's get that leg seen to, an' then I'll get John," Aunt Máire says, never letting go of Red's shoulder and arm.

Red falls fast asleep the moment Aunt Máire sews the last stitch in his leg.

In his dreams, Red relives their passage after the trip to Cavan, from the town where Ellen and John had hidden. Ellen spoke of her own demons. She had a bad feeling the British would eventually tie her to her grandfather who'd slain two soldiers with his iron pike and had gotten away with it for years. Either way, due to her affiliation with Red, she was condemned. But who *wasn't* doomed in Ireland? Ellen was with her grandparents the night they came for her grandfather. For any negative encounters she, Red and John might have had or would ever have with British soldiers, Ellen secretly blamed herself because of her grandfather's actions, although they were, as they were reared to believe, always in self-defence. Had she known of Red's killing of the soldier who murdered his Da, she might have been willing to share the blame. But he never spoke of that to anyone. Not until he was an old man living in Cooper's Cove, Newfoundland.

"Remember Neddy," whispers Aunt Máire, even though she knows her nephew is sound asleep, "never trust the horns of a bull, the heels of a horse, or the smile of an Englishman."

As audibly as she would ever dare, for fear of drawing unwanted attention, Aunt Máire cries herself to sleep. The ancient urge to keen in great shrieks of dreadfulness knocks hard against her aching heart and soul.

# CHAPTER NINE

## *Ireland, 1778*

Two weeks have passed since Red slain the two soldiers in the hills beyond Galway City. Just when Red thought he was healing, the gunshot wound to his leg became terribly infected. Due to the large loss of blood, Aunt Máire first thought gangrene was beginning to set in. But no drastic change of colour occurred on Red's injured leg. She'd removed the musket ball successfully and finally the tissue and broken skin around the wound began healing. But the getting better didn't happen quickly enough for Red. It wasn't until four days later he could stand long enough without the pressure and pain causing him to nearly faint. Unless Ellen had been treated for her wound, he knew the chances of her being alive were slim. The extra four days' waiting have been the hardest four days of Red's life. Having witnessed more than his share of murdered corpses, Red dreads the possibilities which lie before him. But a glimmer of hope reminds him Ellen is strong and perhaps her innate warmness has brought out the best in the British soldiers to whom she's enslaved.

Red is leaving to head back up through the hills again. He leans to one side, keeping weight off his bandaged, injured leg. John is still crying continuously over his absent mother, though his tears are often replaced with questions multiplying constantly. Both Red and Aunt Máire fret over unleashing the situation's realm of possible realities to the boy. The child has heard of death, even seen dead birds and the odd cat and dog rotting on travels with his father and mother, but such thoughts of his dear Mammy in such a state, and never coming back, his five-year-old mind can hardly grasp.

Galway, all of a sudden, seems to breathe a little easier. More people dare stepping outdoors in daylight; some wearing smiles their faces had long since forgotten or never knew existed. All this because of the war in America. Minutemen there, ordinary citizens fighting for their freedom against the British Crown, are making it increasingly difficult for England to regain control, and more troops are needed from this side of the Atlantic to fight there.

Visibly-absent numbers of British troops in Ireland lends an odd air of support to local freedom fighters. England, aware the war in America is also fueling demands from the people of Ireland, cringe at the possibility of another mass uprising here. It's a good time for Red to take advantage of this opportunity to find Ellen and take her home. Or to bury her remains, give her a proper Christian burial.

Just as Red is about to leave, a knock comes to the door. Red hides in the back room while Aunt Máire answers the door. The visitor is an old friend of the family. Aunt Máire invites him to enter her home. Knowing Red is in a rush to leave, she doesn't waste time offering the man tea.

"What's the matter, Adrian?" Aunt Máire asks. "Is it eggs ya needs?"

"No, Mah-ree," the man answers. "I'm terribly sorry t' bodder you, Mah-ree, but I heared a woman's corpse has been discovered some miles distant, up in the hills. An' I heared what went on wit' yer nephew an' the Brits. An' everyone is right proud o' him for what he done, but terribly sad if 'tis his poor wife that's up there like that."

Red has heard every word, and can't stand it no longer. He comes out of the room, into the little kitchen.

The visitor, Adrian, is startled. He stands, cap in hand.

104

"I mean no disrespect, Edward," the man says stammering. "I knew yer Da. He was the finest o' men."

"'Tis alright," Red says, taking a deep breath. "We're glad ya came by wit' that information. I have t' go."

Red gives Aunt Máire a quick kiss on the cheek, puts his cap on his head and leaves.

Aunt Máire sighs, shakes her head, and makes the sign of the cross over her breast.

"I hope I didn't," Adrian begins before Aunt Máire raises a hand to hush him

"Ya did what ya were 'sposed t' do, Adrian, an' we're grateful ya came by."

Aunt Máire walks to the door and opens it - a sign for the man to take his leave. She is glad John is in the barn and was out of range to hear the man's news. Adrian enters the yard, puts his cap back on his head without a word and leaves.

Aunt Máire silently prays the corpse isn't Ellen; that, somehow, it would be best if Red never finds her. Having witnessed the change for the worse in him after his father's death, she can just imagine how he'd be after seeing the body of his dead wife.

On the long, rocky path out through Aunt Máire's property, Adrian passes Red who's is stopped and talking to a young man. He nods to both men while passing them.

"'Tis all set, Mr. Houlihan," the young man says under his breath.

"T'anks, Michael," Red returns in whisper.

There are just a handful of British soldiers left between Galway City and the hills above. In town, they are easily distracted by a group of young fellows willing to help Red through this, his worst plight since Da's sickening death so long ago. The lads stage a big fight near the Italian Arch on the quay, and the soldiers, already nervous due to the absence of their counterparts normally quadrupling in numbers, are there in short order. The saucy Galway boys taunt the soldiers, making fun of their strange dialects.

"Wonderful!" a soldier says, with perfect sarcasm Red says could only be delivered by an Englishman. "The next generation of Rebels; just what we need."

The Irish boys seriously consider attacking the soldiers and pushing them into the water, but were aptly warned by Michael and others not to say or do anything more than create a minor disturbance on Red's behalf. Another group of lads hanging out in Galway City's east end are in place and ready to do the same should other soldiers make their way towards the woods where Red is headed.

The Irish lads at the Italian Arch accuse each other of certain family members denouncing Catholicism and turning Protestant so they would solely inherit their fathers' land when they die. One of the soldiers is impressed with the youngsters' knowledge of the new law set forth by the British Crown, and encourages his fellow soldiers to let the boys fight it out. Born thespians, the Irish boys give it their all and their audience is far from disappointed. The soldiers, some not much older than the acting boys, are relieved to have a bit of light entertainment in the absence of their far-more-serious superior-ranking officers.

"The French, sidin' wit' the Americans," Michael says to Red, "are still t'reatenin' t' invade England, an' possibly the nort' o' Ireland."

"I haven't seen the Journal in a few days," Red says. "What else did they write?"

Michael takes a crumpled Hibernian Journal from his pocket, unravels it and sits against a big rock alongside the road. He clears his throat.

"It says that this situation has the backs o' Ireland's Protestants up, too," Michael reads. "They're already after marchin' in Dublin wit' demonstrations, threatenin' a rebellion o' their own. Now, most o' the British troops not sent t' fight in Amerikay have been ordered t' Dublin."

"Jaysus, what are they hopin' t' accomplish there?" Red says.

"…ordered t' Dublin," Michael reads from the paper, "where it is hoped their presence will quell the risin' tempers an' frustrations o' the nervous public."

"T'anks, Michael," Red says. "Yer a good man."

With this latest update on the state of affairs in Ireland, and with the young lads keeping the British soldiers busy with their acting and taunting, now seems an ideal opportunity, the only chance, for Red to begin closure to his nightmare.

"Alright, Michael," Red says, "stay outta harm's way, an' keep me abreast o' what's happenin' 'round these parts 'til I gets through this mess."

"I will, Mr. Houlihan."

Michael folds the newspaper and shoves it into his pocket. He stares at the ground for a few moments, then turns to Red.

"I hope ya finds yer wife, Sir."

"T'anks, Michael."

"At least we had Mammy t' bury," Michaels says, sobbing. "I can't imagine what you an' little John are feelin'."

"I've t' go, Michael," Red says, unable to talk about what happened to Ellen. "I've t' go."

"'Kay," Michael says. "'Kay."

Michael wipes tears from his face, nods to Red and turns away.

"Michael!" Red says.

"Yes, Sir?"

"I'll say a prayer fer yer Mudder, an' all yer family."

"T'anks, Mr. Houlihan. That means a lot t' all o' us," Michael says. "I'll be sure an' tell Da ya said so."

Red nods to Michael as Michael turns and heads in through a grown-over woods' path. Red walks about a hundred feet on the main roadway and stops. He opens the leather bag hanging around his body and unfastens the copper button keeping it closed. He takes out a small, but fancy canteen, twists the cork from the opening and puts the canteen to his lips. He takes three big gulps of poteen before forcing the cork plug on a tiny chain back into the canteen. He stares at the emblem embossed on one side of the canteen, shakes his head in disgust and shoves the container back into his carrying bag. He hastens his steps until he reaches another side road - one leading to an old stable.

The alcohol helps take the edge off the pain from Red's injured leg, as he carefully manouveurs around rocks left protruding from the earth by heavy rain. When he reaches the stable, Bolg hears him and snorts in anticipation of seeing his master again. Red wastes no time untying Bolg from a post and opening the gate of the stall where the horse has been staying. Red kisses his horse between the eyes and leads him outside. Bolg pulls his head back and whinnies at the sight of his master's shaved face.

"Nevermind now, me friend," Red says. "It'll grow again."

Red tosses his head at the fact he's telling Bolg about his beard, as he walks the horse out of the stable. He ties Bolg to an old post outside and goes back inside where he takes a saddle from the wall. He heads back out through the small building's opening where the doors have long since fallen off.

While fastening the saddle to Bolg, Red thinks he hears Ellen's voice, then realizes she is too far away for that to be possible.

"Don't be scared now," he says to the horse. "'Tis still me, old Fella."

Red takes the dress and bandanna from his carrying bag and puts on the garments. Bolg grunts at the sight.

"I know, b'y," Red says.

Red mounts Bolg and the two head off through the woods and onto a city side street where people are going about their chores. He expects snickers, even comments, from the few people he passes alongside the road, but not a sound is uttered. Or at least not heard. Their silence tells Red they're well aware of his plight. Within half an hour Red and Bolg are past the city and onto a path which will join onto the one where Red hopes to find Ellen.

Although he's been warned of the stench, Red wears no garment to cover his big nose. Bolg trudges mournfully along, making several attempts to turn back down the hill, but Red keeps him in line. Each time it taps off Bolg's faded-brown leather saddle, the four-foot spade makes a dull sound. It echoes through Red's ears fluttering with absolute madness. Inescapable exasperation. The opportunity to bury Da never happened, and the shovel hasn't been used for such a cause in the years since. At least not for someone belonged to him. Each time the spade reverberates, it triggers memories of each night Red crept and crawled to the wooded area outside the open space where Da's body lay in a rotting heap.

No British soldiers are in sight, nor encampment sites showing where they've been. Although it's what Red has been hoping for, the absence of soldiers likely means the absence of Ellen. Or at least, worse again, the presence of her without life. He braces himself for the worst.

To spare himself extra moments in the presence of Ellen's corpse, Red halts Bolg a hundred feet or so from where he's been told she might be. From the sack tied onto Bolg's saddle, Red warily removes the dress Aunt Máire carefully folded and packed - the same dress Ellen wore when she and Red exchanged wedding vows in secret on a cold, foggy night along a river, about ten miles northwest of here. The priest, an old friend of the Houlihan's, once from Inis Meáin himself, held a lantern in one hand, and read from a Bible in the other. It was too perilous to include anyone else, for fear the English might learn of Catholics practicing their own religion. Red always joked Bolg was his best man, the soul witness to the pair's exchanging of matrimonial vows. Ellen was more beautiful than Red had ever seen her. He told her, no matter what, he'd always profess his love for her.

Following their wedding, their clandestine journey back to Galway through paths chartered occasionally by foreign men and their hunting dogs ensured a few scratches and scrapes to the skin, *and* a tear or two in Ellen's dress. She was hardly amused at the garment's imperfections thereafter, but never bothered mending small rips from tree branches on the narrow trails. It was all part of their romantic experience, and she expected nothing less than such roughness from the likes of her ruggedly-handsome man. After a family blessing from Aunt Máire, and a lovely supper of fresh lamb and potatoes, the newly-wedded couple consummated their love and marriage in the hay-filled loft of the big barn out back. Lost in a soothing melody from Red's wooden whistle, Ellen hoped and prayed the night would last forever. Nights such as that one would be repeated once they found themselves a peaceful place to live, Red assured his bride. Ellen believed him, silently longing to one day take passage to that magical place across the ocean. Newfoundland. As she lay in a bed of new hay, wrapped only in a colourful knitted blanket - a present from Aunt Máire - Ellen drifted off to sleep. John was born nine months later, in August 1773.

From his living nightmare, Red's stoic countenance collapses. Tears born of those innocent, exquisite memories of his wife sprinkle over the garment he holds to his nose and lips. Phantom smells fill his senses - the flowers Ellen wore in her hair and on her dress on their wedding night. He tethers Bolg's harness strap to an elm tree. Torn between love and hatred, he chooses love, carefully laying the dress over the saddle. Red says there's no need for both of them to see whatever there is to see. The old horse nuzzles his big head into Red's neck and shoulder, snorting his disapproval. His master cups him behind an ear, pulling his face into Bolg's. Eye to eye, a moment of silence occurs before Red again bursts into tears. Bolg hauls away from Red, tugging at the leather strap tied to the tree. He snorts and stomps his displeasure again until his master hushes him with a light slap across the head. Red unties the sheet of rolled-up sail cloth fastened to the saddle straps and heads up the path.

If she's really there, Ellen will be wrapped in the sturdy cloth and, once back to Aunt Máire's yard, carefully washed with water.

Aunt Máire will clothe Ellen in her wedding dress, and young Michael will transport the body by horse and wagon to the beach. There, he'll wait for Red in his currach rowed there by a friend and tied amongst the hookers at the quay. Once in the boat, Red will row or sail, depending on the amount of wind, the twenty-five miles back to Inis Meáin. A makeshift, padded-with-horsehair sling attached to Da's block and tackle will carry Ellen's body over the cliffs and the poor soul will receive a dignified burial not far from their house - one in which they were never able to properly settle and consider home.

Red is less than forty feet from Bolg when an awful stench hits his nose. Weakness overtakes him again and he falls to his knees, purging and bawling hot tears - sobbing from the bottom of his broken soul for his sweetheart. Part of him prays it isn't Ellen. But, in his heart, he knows it is her. He has no appetite and hasn't eaten in days. Nothing but a little bit of water comes from his insides. He's unsure if the great pangs in his guts are from hunger or hurt. He gets up, forcing his good leg ahead of the bad along the path of mud and stones.

After another forty or fifty feet, the stink engulfs him altogether. The buzz of flies is as disturbing as the thought of what lies ahead. To his right, about ten feet away, a colour unnatural to the normal green and reddish surroundings stands out. When he reaches it, his worst fears are confirmed. Plans for a suitable burial for his darling wife vanish immediately. He wants to scream, but that might attract unwelcomed company. If Redcoats turn up, surely he'll murder the lot of them. Somehow, through the grace of God, he has reserved enough common sense to consider John's life and both their futures. So far. He prays for strength to remain quiet, to treat the situation as practically as possible. No time to let his mind run wild. That can come later.

Red returns to Bolg and unlatches the spade linked by chain

to the saddle bag. As if the horse knows the emotional magnitude of what Red has seen, Bolg stops snorting and moving about. The horse's eyes turn glassy. His head droops. Red gives him a pat and rub on the neck before leaving again. Disregarding his bold pride, Red ties two colourful handkerchiefs tightly around his face, just above his nose and across his chin. The last thing he needs is to contract sickness or disease.

"Ellen's soul is free," he tries to convince himself.

This thought brings a short-lived comfort to the grieving husband, enabling him strength to carry on. Finish what he's started.

Ellen's skin is ashen, laced with marks of black, purple and blue. She is lying on her side, almost naked. Crows have taken her eyes, the sockets now home to crawling insects. Dark brown streaks running down and around her thighs and knees show the soldiers have raped and tortured her before, perhaps even after, she died. Red has ridden past dead women before and as bad as he'd felt for the poor souls, he's never known the depths of hurt shrouding him now.

Fighting to accept Ellen is safe at last, at peace in Heaven with the Lord, Red mechanically starts ripping away fallen wood and shrubs from the ground. He can't bear to put Ellen's body, what's left of it, onto the canvas and then dig. So, he lets it be until a hole, a little more than four feet deep, is dug. Each time the spade hits the earth, he curses the Brits. Curses God.

When he's done digging what he feels is a big enough hole for Ellen, he dares to look at her body again. He glances quickly and closes his eyes. Even though her body is battered and lifeless, Red feels overwhelmingly remorseful at the notion of letting her go from his sight again, of letting her go. Forever. It is too much to take. He asks God's forgiveness for cursing Him. Then prays aloud for Ellen's soul to have a safe seat in Heaven, and for The Lord to forgive him for leaving her and for not being able to save her. He uses his dirty arms to wipe the stream of tears from his eyes so he may see better what he has to do. He picks up the spade again and places it gently against Ellen's corpse. He's scared the metal will puncture her skin, cause her further misery. He turns his head away and applies pressure to the shovel in both his hands until the decomposing body is on the canvas he's spread on the grass.

A small hole in the back of Ellen's dress, and a dark-red/blackish stain around and trailing away from it, are evidence of where the musket ball lodged into her body. In his mind, Red hears the *slap* again and shutters. His instinct is to remove the ball, take it to the forge for melting into another weapon or bullet, but there's no need. She's suffered indignity enough. Again, he hopes she died soon after falling off the horse, and perhaps the voice he thought was hers was all in his head. Or maybe one of the soldiers is as adept as himself at mimicking voices. It no longer matters. She's gone. Red takes an edge of the canvas, tucking it under her side, then rolls the body until it is wrapped as well as can be. A stream of sweat trickles from between his eyes, over his nose and onto the canvas.

His heart too frozen to send tears to his eyes, Red ponders the past two weeks - imagining himself giving Ellen one last kiss, to say goodbye, that they'd meet again. His last kiss would have to be the one he gave her, on the forehead, as her lips turned blue, then white, just before she fell off the horse. He drags the canvas into the hole and, with the limited strength he possesses, gets out quickly as possible. He covers his Love with dirt and rocks until the land above her body is close to level again.

On his knees, Red extends both his arms, sweeping them madly to organize the dirt pile the best he can, just the way Ellen would have done in her particular fashion. Rain. Letting his head fall into the dirt and mud, a prayer is whispered while his tears mix with the quickly-gathering downpour. Red throws sticks, sods and unearthed shrubs over the grave. He stands straight, spade in hand, and walks with a strange, fresh sense of pride; a closure of sorts, perhaps, back down the hill to Bolg.

Now willing to face anyone daring to face him, Red sheds the clothes he'd worn in disguise. The rain keeps enemy soldiers inside and he makes it back to Aunt Máire's without incident.

Inside the house, Red unleashes all the pain-filled emotion he'd kept pent up for the past several days. Into his son's shoulder, he screeches loudly. Little John asks no questions, only hugs his father. Aunt Máire falls to her knees on the dirt floor and goes into a litany of prayers for Ellen's soul and all the souls of Irish men, women and children who have suffered and died at the callous hands of the British.

# DARRELL DUKE

# CHAPTER TEN

## *Three Weeks Later*

## *Ireland, 1778*

A quick change of the wind and the stench it carries turns Red's stomach. Both master and horse smell it long before they see it. Another rotting body. When the corpse comes into view, the path, what's left of the old road, isn't wide enough to avoid it altogether. Red leans to the left, just enough so his face doesn't strike the hard branches of ancient trees lining the sides of the old-world stony carriageway. The horse does the same.

"Troops not long past," Red says of the dusty air.

The smell and sight of a corpse inevitably takes Red's mind back to the day he found Ellen's body. The three weeks since for him have consisted of maddening nervous breakdowns, but ones, somehow, controlled in their timing. Red still had to see John and spend valuable time with him, even though Aunt Máire was, and still is, there for them both. When it came time for John to find sleep, Red would walk to the stable where Bolg waited. There, Red screamed his anger, ripped wood from the walls and threw whatever he could manage to lift in an effort to relieve his body of the magnitudes of bad energy accumulated from a lifetime of madness. But more so from the past month or more since Ellen was shot. Over and over he relived their conversations which, in hindsight, he realizes were mainly one-sided; his opinion, on how things should be. There is guilt over that, and always will be. Every time he closes his eyes, he sees her - the lovely, sparkling eyes. Then the endless holes where her eyes used to be - and he reaches his hands out to touch her, to fix her, to breathe life back into her battered and abused body. After eight or nine days, he and Bolg made the trip he feared the most - to tell the dreadful news to Ellen's father and mother in Roscommon.

When Red arrived at their door, it wasn't the absence of their daughter on horseback with her husband which told the tale, but his long face. Ellen's father fought hard not to strike Red, but ultimately he understood the nature of the never-ending war with the British and that not everyone could or would escape with their lives intact, no matter their involvement, or sometimes lack thereof, in this fruitless battle for a morsel of freedom. Ellen's mother wasn't so understanding, and nor did Red expect her to be. She pounded her fists against his face, chest and arms until she collapsed in grief upon the muddy ground. Red, nor the father, made an effort to stop her. Red took the hard blows. She had every right, they all knew.

"Ye may travel t' Galway when yeer ready," Red told them, "t' see John. He'll be expecting ye."

Red apologized again before mounting Bolg and riding away.

Now, faced with what he feels is a personal responsibility, Red tries to lock away the events of the past while to get through this latest atrocity, literally, hanging before him.

He slows Bolg's trot to do the unavoidable; turn back towards the body. No blood drips from it and Red knows *it* - he - isn't long there. Probably still alive. No. There'd be no smell like this. Unless. He takes a deep breath before sticking his neck forward, staring into the woods. Squinting his eyes for a closer look, he swallows hard. At least one source of the stink is revealed.

Through thick foliage, Red sees another man; hung, too, maybe less than a week before. The muscle and flesh of the dead man's legs stop just below the knees, as far as wild dogs and wolves could jump and reach with their powerful jaws. A bloody shoe remains on one leg. On the other, nothing but bare bones scraped clean by sharp teeth and licked dry.

As much as he'd like to, Red can't close his eyes. Before he's finishing blessing himself, he sees another body. In the light wind, it moves slightly. The weight of the corpses hung with rope cause the branches of the old trees to creak and moan. The reek clings tightly to every particle of the summer air. The second body: same condition. No legs below the knees. The British have gone through great measure, hanging each body the same height from the ground; no doubt on purpose, to feed wild dogs that would, otherwise, be bothering the soldiers on their incessant travels around the country. No shoe on this one: a woman, too far away to determine her age. Streaks of dried blood mark each corpse's face where birds have taken the eyes. Again, Red has vivid flashbacks of Ellen's corpse, the state of her body and once-beautiful face.

Bolg shivers and begins to buck a little, urging Red to hurry. He tries to move toward the freshly-hung man. Before turning the horse to face the stranger, Red hops to the ground, buckles over and throws up the scanty contents of his guts. Shaking his head does nothing to rid the horrible smell.

A fresh breeze turns the body, as Red is startled by a strange sound. The man is still alive. Yet unable to form a word. The sudden stirring of the legs not yet eaten by wild animals drags Red and the horse toward him in a hurry. Red had been told his uncle survived a hanging, having been told a secret by an older Irishman when he was younger - before clashes with the enemy, should he be caught - of a certain way he could move his body and force his neck downward towards the noose, adding resistance to the force of the great blow that has killed thousands of Irish men, women and children in the six-hundred and eleven years since adversaries first invaded here. But Red figures it was nothing but pure luck and God's good grace if anyone survived a hanging. The knot on this fellow has, obviously, been tied wrongly, in a hurry.

Red springs from his horse and, despite the ancient belief that it is bad luck to go beneath a hangman's noose, comes up under the man with both his arms outstretched. Standing on his toes, he raises his body higher than its normal six feet. There's a loose rock by the roadside, one he might be able to roll and use to attain greater height, but he's afraid to leave his position - wary his efforts to save the man will be more useless than any remaining chance.

Red's whiskery face pushes against the midsection of the dying man, as he slowly drags the top of his head and face along the man's tattered, wet and bloodstained clothes. Physical signs of centuries-old hatred - bayonet wounds - cover the remains of the man's woolen shirt. Small amounts of blood spurt from the man's side. Red is afraid to lessen his grip, yet he's unsure if he's quickening the process of the poor man's death with his weight against the hemorrhaging body.

"Cowards," he says to himself. "Stabbin' a man hangin' wit' his hands tied behind 'im."

Quick jabs they'd been, from a soldier or two as they left on their horses. No deep wounds or twists of the blade.

The awful sound comes again from the dry throat of the man, and Red is careful not to let him drop the slightest. Red's body trembles from the encumbrance. He moves his head around the injured man, making sure no one is coming. The body jerks, as Red's eyes finally meet the victim's.

"Jaysus Christ, Brendan!" Red says in a load whisper. "*Mo dheartháir* (My brother)!"

Tears stream from Red's eyes, his breath now three times as laboured, as his feet scramble for a way to raise his brother higher. A cut below Brendan's bruised and swollen left eye further enrages Red.

"Hold on, Bren! Jaysus, hold on. Please, Dear Lord. Let 'im hold on!"

Brendan tries to speak again.

Red cautiously slides his left arm down to Brendan's upper left leg, taking the weight of his younger brother, then grabs a knife from his pouch.

"Hold on, Bren!" Red grunts, "Yer gonna be alright. Yer gonna be alright! *Fillean meal ar an meallaire*! (Evil returns to the evil doer)," Red swears.

Red reaches up and holds the sharp steel of his blade against the rope hauling the last bit of life out of his little brother. He saws at the rope, cutting through it quickly, and also into Brendan's neck a little in the process. The new flesh wound bleeds, as Brendan falls like a boulder to the hard road. Red's hand, too, is sliced and bleeding from the handle-less knife.

The moment the rope is off Brendan's neck, both men hear growls and heavy breathing. Wild dogs. The old horse is quiet no longer, as he whinnies and snorts, kicking his hind legs at the dogs trying to latch onto its large quarters. One of the savages receives a swift blow from a hoof and is sent tumbling across the ground. The animal, half wolf, half dog, drags itself to the base of a large tree, yelping, unable to rejoin his comrades in the attack. Blood trickles from one of its ears and another dog is there in moments, lapping it up, sniffing for the internal wound it can't see.

"Hold on, Bren! Hold on!" Red says, kicking loose pebbles and dust from the road.

The dogs close in, anxious to taste fresh blood. Red curses the dogs before throwing one of his blades. One of the scrawny animals lets out a yelp, then falls silent from an accurate blow. The blade passes through its emaciated body, skittering two or three feet along the road. Bolg runs half a circle around the remaining two blood-thirsty hounds still growling, furious from hunger and the exhilaration of the hunt. Red draws another blade from the leather belt case around his waist and holds it to the left of his head. With no time to linger, he takes aim and lets the blade fly. A dog screeches, as the blade enters its stomach, what's there of it, leaving a visible tear.

The injured beast stumbles towards Red, still growling, its shrunken guts revealed and hanging through torn flesh. Blood drips in quick succession to the ground. A deathly blow from one of Red's tattered boots, ones stolen from a dead English soldier, lands on the side of the dog's head, relieving it of its misery. The remaining dog whimpers while sniffing the dead one closest to Red. It growls weakly before taking off into the woods where the bodies are hanging. Almost silently, it runs back to the road. Red is sure it will make another attempt at taking a bite of his brother, but suddenly it stops. Half crouching, the dog looks in the direction from which Red and Bolg rode, before bolting back into the woods.

"Shhhh!" Red tells Brendan, reaching for a canteen in the rawhide bag hanging from the horse's saddle.

He cups Brendan's neck, titling it back slightly, letting drops of water hit his brother's blue lips.

"'Tis alright," Red says, looking to Bolg.

The horse settles a bit.

"Don't try an' talk yet," Red says to his brother, increasing the amount of water with each pour. "Hold on. Hold on, ya stubborn imbecile!"

When Brendan finally swallows, he begins to choke. Red turns him on his side to let him vomit.

Looking to the other side of the road, Red sees another body. And another. And another. The smell seems worse. Red takes advantage of his brother's position to cut the rope keeping Brendan's hands behind his back. With Brendan turned over, Red's about to give him another drop of water, but stops.

"Listen!" he orders, as if Brendan had a say in the sounds he was making. "That's why the dog ran away."

The thumping of hooves from several horses shakes the earth. The enemy isn't far away.

"Where, in the name, o' God, did, ya, get, it?" Brendan manages to ask.

"Where do ya think?" Red says, pointing a finger at the canteen sporting an embossed emblem of the British Crown. "Now, don't let me hear ya open yer gob again. Hold on!"

Red hauls out small pieces of cloth, runs to the nearest tree and cuts into the bark with a knife. He rubs the cloths along the fresh slits and returns to Brendan.

"Now, take a deep breath, hold it in, an' be quiet!" Red orders.

"*Nach eil i fuar* (Isn't it cold)?" Brendan says of the air.

"I said, *Dún do bhéal!* (Shut your mouth)!"

Red lifts what's left of Brendan's shirt, and presses the cloths sticky with sap over two bayonet wounds. Brendan sucks air through his teeth, his eyes rolling back from the pain, as Red temporarily dresses the bayonet gashes.

"Good lad," Red says quietly. "Now, anyplace else I need t' look at 'fore we go?"

"Not that I can feel," Brendan says with a big sigh.

"I'll do a better job o' fixin' ya up once we gets a chance t' stop an' rest."

Red leans into his brother, lifts him to his feet, then shoves him up sideways across the horse. Red hurriedly apologizes for the route he's about to take while giving Bolg a swift kick. The horse is driven through the trees and, eventually, onto an old path where Red presumes the British won't bother to look.

With the reigns twisted tightly around both his hands, Red presses on his brother's back. Afraid Brendan might die if he falls asleep, Red incessantly encourages him to stay awake, saying it won't be long before they can stop and eat. Thoughts of someone stabbing his little brother cause his blood to boil again, and Bolg receives a harder kick. *They like to let you suffer, the British, and would never give you a quick death. Not if they can help it*, Red thinks. The leaves and branches scraping and poking at Brendan's body bring from him new moans of misery.

Now and then larks fly up from the seldom-used path. They've no time for singing, only for getting out of harm's way. Tall trees lining the old road keep the fluttering birds out of the sight of English soldiers who, surely, must now be upon the spot where Brendan was hung.

"Ya had no business at that meetin', Bren!" Red scorns.

"Jaysus! Tipperary, Bren? Jaysus! I know they're part o' Ireland, but we've our own t' worry 'bout in the meantime, don't ya think?"

Red is really cross, and conscious of the fact his calling Brendan out will give his brother something else to cling to, besides thoughts of dying.

"When they told me you were goin', Bren, I said, 'Goddamn it! He could've at least let me know.' Yer all I got, Bren, for Jaysus' sake. Have a bitta sense, b'y! Think o' poor Mam."

When Bolg breaks out of the wooded path, the air is heavenly. An open field with freshly-cut hay spread to dry brings false warmth to their souls. No road nearby. The main thoroughfare veered off to the right a couple of miles back. The threat of being caught seems distant or at least delayed, and Red says *whoa* to the old horse.

Lying in the shade of giant rhubarb leaves, Red nurses his younger brother with lukewarm water from his other canteen, then with poteen from the enemy's. Slowly, Brendan chews the morsels of bread Red feeds him. After an hour or so he receives Red's permission to try and speak.

"Do ya t'ink the Druids held their masses in places like this, Neddy?" Brendan asks Red with sleepy, childlike excitement in his voice. "The sacrificin'?"

"No one knows much 'bout them, Bren," Red says. "What might be mythical t' us was normal t' them, I'm sure. Now, never mind the Druids an' tell me why ya came t' Tipperary!"

Brendan tries to clear his throat while extending his hand toward Red. Red holds the canteen to his brother's lips while Brendan takes another drink of water.

"Lads in Ballinasloe," Brendan begins, coughing to clear his throat. "They said that the soldiers who killed....I mean, shot, who took....Ellen....Jaysus, I'm sorry, Neddy. I should'na said that."

"'Tis alright, Bren. 'Tis alright, go on." Red is dying to tell of his own misadventure, finding Ellen's body, but decides to wait.

"The lads, Neddy, I heard 'em talkin' 'bout what happened an' how the soldiers were makin' a mock'ry o' *you*...called ya a coward they did, an' how Ellen..."

Brendan breaks down in tears.

"'Tis alright, Bren, I said. I need t' hear what ya have t' say."

Brendan dabs his eyes with his dirty shirt sleeve and sucks air through the gap in his front teeth again, helping ease the pain in his ribs. He exhales slowly before speaking again.

"They were drunk an' celebratin' the gettin' rid of anudder o' us, Neddy, they said. The Irish. We've no chance, Neddy!"

"Jaysus, Bren, finish yer goddamn story, will ya!"

"The lads were hidin' behind a stone wall when two soldiers were fallin' up the road drunk, arms draped over a couple o' local girls, braggin' how they'd made 'way wit' the wife o' Rebel Red Houlihan. They said ya ran them down an' how they shoulda shot you an' yer family before ya had a chance t' raise the horse an' trample them in the first place. One o' them bastards ya rode down is sent t' the infirmary, Neddy, wit' broken ribs an' somet'ing else...an' they've upped the price on yer head."

"No odds 'bout that, Bren!" Red says, impatient to hear why his little brother was where he was and what had happened.

"That's why, Neddy. That's why!" Brendan pleads. "They said

they were headin' this way in two days, after the young girls made a bargain wit' 'em, t' keep the bastards away from their own families."

"Same ole story," Red says.

"The young girls," Brendan continues, "they knows everyt'ing, Neddy....who's holdin' the meetins an' where they'll be held. 'Tis nuttin' safe anymore!"

"Nuttin's ever been safe here, Bren," Red assures him. "Now! Anyt'ing else?"

"The soldier doin' all the gabbin' said he's the wan shot Ellen, an' how he'll shoot a hundred more Irish at the meetin' here in Tipperary if given the chance. We never even made an effort t' fight 'em, Neddy. We were just talkin' 'bout what we might be able t' do when they showed up, how we might be able t' join forces t' win a bit o' freedom one day Neddy, that's all. Same t'ings everyone's always talked 'bout 'round here, right. Some o' the lads were shot. Don't know if they lived or died. When I heared gun shots, I stopped. I musta been struck in the head wit' the butt of a gun or a stick from behind. When I came to, they were raisin' me up in the tree. Wasn't a proper hangman's knot or else I'd be dead. They musta had someplace else t' be in a hurry 'cause they wasted no time torturin' us, t'ank God. A few they took with 'em. Fer what I don't know."

"There's too much land between home an' Tipperary, Bren! We can't make friends wit' the whole o' Ireland. There's too many hungry men willin' t' spake an' too many girls an' women willing t' lie down wit' the English fer the false promise of a bit o' safety."

"I know, Neddy, I know. But I got a good mem'ry o' the fella in me head, what he looks like, the one who said he shot poor Ellen,...an' I've 'nough lads t' trust down here who would've helped me find a way t' make away wit' 'im. We'd planned t' have our meetin' an' deal wit' that sliveen afterwards."

"Forget that, Bren!" Red raises his voice, then goes quiet again. "Every goddamn soldier o' the British army took Ellen from me an' John. They'll all pay an' there'll be no discrimination on my part. A Redcoat is a Redcoat! Remember what I said - *Fillean meal ar an meallaire.* (Evil returns to the evil doer)."

"But, Neddy!"

"Now, you listen here!" Red's voice is raised again and ridden with anger. "One by one we'll get rid o' the English. An' bit by bit we'll have control of our lives an' our land. But we still have t' play by *their* rules, as long as they're lookin' *our* way. We'll worship Pope Pius, pray t' God an' Jesus, sing our songs, tell our stories to our children an' do whatever else we feel we must do t' keep *our* Ireland alive....if only in our hearts an' minds, Bren, until we figures a way t' send every British soldier the hell home out of it. But, until then, we can only do what we like when they're *not lookin' our way.* An' that's a rare occasion, we know. T' do otherwise is pure stupidity!"

"I'm sorry, Neddy. I am," Brendan cries. "I was just...." Red interrupts.

"How do ya feel, Bren?" Red asks.

"*Dobhránta* (Stupid)."

"No, b'y, how's yer wounds? Can ya hold on another spell, 'til we makes a bit more headway?"

"I can," Brendan says.

"'Cause we have t' save our breat', an' take advantage o' the moon's light. No need o' sayin' more. Just don't let me hear tell o' ya strayin' so far from home again, 'tis all. 'Tis the traitors we have t' look out fer, Bren. Don't be so sure ya can trust people just 'cause ya knows 'em. Someone who waved an' smiled at me an' Ellen an' John passin' through Longford ran like an amadan t' the Brits. I'll find out who t'was. The situation is worse ev'ry day wit' the English tellin' all kinds o' foolishness an' lies t' the locals, lookin' fer their support, now that the Spanish are out t' get 'em, too."

"I won't, Neddy, I won't," Brendan whispers, laying his head across his big brother's lap. "T'anks, Neddy. T'anks a lot."

"Someone handed me a copy o' the *Hibernian Journal* when I was in Cavan, before...." Red's voice begins to crack. He clears his throat with a drop of water from the canteen. "The crowd in London are panickin' over their self-inflicted crisis in Amerikay, Bren. Leaders o' their government on this side are dyin' an' disappearin', desertin' their posts. An' gaps are appearin' here wit' regards t' the numbers o' troops in Ireland, creatin' opportunities fer us. Ya should get away, Bren, while ya can. Change yer name. Sign up wit' their forces an' tell 'em ya wants t' fight fer their King, t' help straighten out the heathens amongst 'em in Amerikay. Tell 'em what they wants t' hear, *dearthair beag* (little brother)."

"But, Neddy!" Brendan is quickly hushed by Red's hand.

"Get yer free passage 'cross the ocean. Kill an Englishman or two fer show when ya gets there, if it comes down t' that, an' get the hell outta there....on one o' them boats headin' north t' Upper or Lower Canada or Newf'undland. They're still English, the crowd in Amerikay, Bren, but like us, they're tryin' t' live their lives the way they wants t' live; not how the King o' England says we all should live. I'm hardly tellin' ya t' join them in *their* fight fer freedom, but Jaysus, Bren, 'tis a way out o' here!"

"What of Mam, then, Neddy?" Brendan asks.

"Mam's alright on Inis Meáin. She's alright 'cause the Brits thinks I lives in Galway, or somewhere handy t' there, an' spends their time lookin' fer me there. Don't worry 'bout her. She'll be fine. Go, Bren, to a post on the other side o' Ireland, in Meat', or Cavan or Dublin even, where they don't know yer face. Sign up an' go, Bren! I got a letter from over there, in Newf'undland - an island, run by the English, but lots o' land t' make yer own, lots o' woods t' say prayers in, an' plenty o' fish t' eat an' sell. Little Placentia is the town's name."

"Hard t' 'magine truth in that," Brendan mumbles. "How would *I* ever find that place?"

"Fishin' boats. Always comin' an' goin' t' Newf'undland, I'm told."

"What if I'm found out, fer desertin'?" Brendan worries.

"Nah!" Red says. "The English are too busy fightin' their own crowd in Amerikay t' worry 'bout a nobody like you. An' the Spanish an' French are not making it too aisey fer 'em, either, t' cross the Atlantic."

"But ya said New-fun-land. Is that how ya says it?"

"Yah!"

"Ya said the English rules that place, too. What'd be the sense in leavin' here an' goin' to anudder place just like it, Neddy?"

"Freedom, Bren! Free-dum!" Red is agitated. "The island there is said t' be endless. Way bigger than Ireland. Endless shoreline. Endless rivers an' loughs. Endless fish. Endless forest. Imagine the fine house ya could make fer yourself wit' no end t' the timber. The English merchants have been there since '13, when they drove the French out o' most of it, I was told. So, what's left o' them are old an' tired an' probably glad t' be away from the politics o' England.

Nothin' stays the same forever, Bren."

"What about their offspring? Wouldn't they be the same as they are here: ignorant, indifferent an' always in yer business?"

"No," Red says, "they've got their eyes or hands on the daughters o' Irishmen who went there t' work fer the merchants. *They* have their own plans. We're all human, Bren, when it comes down to it, an' all any man wants is a good woman wit' youngsters t' pass stories an' songs 'long to."

"I s'pose yer right, Neddy. Gives me somethin' t' t'ink about, anyhow."

"Good!" Red says with little or no expression. "How's yer legs now?"

"Fine, I t'ink."

"'Kay, time t' leave then. Back up ya go."

Red kneels and cups his hands for Brendan to step into. He counts to three and lifts his brother up and across Bolg's broad back. Brendan lets out a yelp from the pain in his ribs.

"Do ya t'ink I could sit up in front o' ya, Neddy, instead o' lyin' 'cross the horse?" Brendan asks. "I'm ugly 'nough wit'out the trees tearin' any more skin off me face than they already have."

"That's true," Red jokes. "As long as ya feels strong 'nough t' sit up."

Red can't help but laugh, as he helps situate his brother in front of him. He then puts his arms around both sides of Brendan and grabs the reigns.

"Hang on," Red says. "Keep yer head t' one side or the other.

An' no more talkin'. You'll need yer strength."

After a few more passes through thickly wooded paths, Red and Brendan and Bolg stop at the River Suir, one of Ireland's Three Sisters. Bolg lowers his head to the running water right away to slake his thrist. The men soon do the same until they feel refreshed. Red and Brendan fall back, taking deep breaths, their minds momentarily astray in the night sky aglow; the highest peaks of the Devil's Bit silhouetted against calming hues of azure, mauve and crimson.

Red lends an arm to his brother. They sit closely, like children again. A steak of moonlight provides a familiar spectacle: breaching trout and salmon. The river is renowned for its fish, especially big salmon. Red gets up.

"Where ya goin' now?" Brendan asks.

"Nowhere."

Red takes a thin, skinned branch tied alongside Bolg's saddle and unwraps twine and a hook from the top of the pole. With his left hand, he lifts a rock and feels around before finding a worm. He works the long, skinny worm over and around the hook, wiping the slime and dirt on the leg of his pants. When he sits on a large, flat stone at the river's edge, Brendan gets up.

"Whatta ya think yer doin'? Red asks.

"Grabbin' some sticks fer the fire."

"Are ya mad?" Red says. "Sit down an' stay down. There'll be no fire this night. You wanna be hung twice in the wan day?"

"Sorry, Neddy!

"'Tis alright, b'y. I'm glad yer alright, Bren. I won't tell Mam 'bout this. She's enough t' worry 'bout, God knows."

"T'anks, Neddy."

"I knows a spot," Red says, "where we can stop an' have a fire t'morrow an' ate the fish. I've berries an' bread. That'll do us till then. Here! Have a swig o' this."

As Red hands Brendan his canteen of liquor, the line of the fishing pole goes taut and, after a long struggle to let the fish tire, Red hauls in the largest salmon either man has ever seen.

"Tell me about Da, Neddy," Brendan pleads in a half-whisper.

"Tell ya wha?" Red answers impatiently.

"What happened to 'im? 'Tis 'bout time ya tells me, Neddy. Jaysus Christ, I've been askin' fer years."

"Like I said a t'ousand times, Bren, I'm not sp'akin' o' it. Ever!"

"Jaysus, Neddy, why not? He was my Da, too."

"Ya don't need t' know the details, Bren! Ya were only a little lad an' were lucky t' have been so - safe at home, on the island, wit' Mam an' the girls." Red's voice turns to a near-cry. "'Tis enough prate now fer one night, Bren! Don't ask me 'bout it again, alright? Never again!"

"But Neddy!"

"Luh, Bren! If Da was here now, he'd be after smackin' the head off ya fer bein' so stupid. Wait! We have t' wait! The Irish must learn t' wait. Observation. *Feighlíocht*, Bren! Vigilance!"

"Wait fer wha?" Bren wants to know. "Wait fer wha? Fer you or me t' be killed? Jaysus, Neddy, ya saved me life again an' I'll never fergit that. But how can we fergit what they did t' Da, whatever they did? Killed 'im. He didn't come home an' I never saw 'im again. That's all I knows. An' why should we fergit what they done t' us an' generations o' us before? Why, Neddy? Why?"

"We're plannin' a big one, Bren," Red assures his little brother. "But there's no hurry. Remember that. No hurry. Wit' the war in Amerikay, England is more divided ev'ry day, an' the French, as much we mightn't like *them*, they're ready t' take on England, too, an' we might have an alibi fer once. We'll keep stealin' guns an' ammunition from the Brits an' buryin' 'em. If we have t' wait anudder twenty years, Bren, we will. We must be prepared. Pray. *Foighne*! (Have patience).

"Yes, b'y, wait 'til 1798. When, Neddy? When?"

"If I knew, I wouldn't even tell ya, Bren. Yer not close t' bein' ready fer a real war. Do what I said! Change yer name fer now an' go join the English fer a free ride t' the udder side o' The Pond. You'll figure it out as ya goes. Ya can always come back if 'tis that bad there."

Just outside the town of *Carraig na Siúire* (Carrick-on-Suir: Rock of the Suir) the next morning, Red leaves Bolg and Brendan in the shield of the woods while he scouts the area for enemy soldiers. From a distance, he sees a Redcoat on either end of the town's three-hundred-year-old stone bridge. He walks cheerily, whistling away, along a well-worn path fringed by tall grass. From down over a lush green bank, Red hears cheerful chatting from what sounds like young girls. The volume of his whistling rises to help introduce his arrival before they see him. The girls look about nine or ten. They're trying to catch trout with their hands.

"Ever hear tell of a fishin' pole?" Red jokes in a low voice. He puts on an extra big smile, keeps his hands in pockets, pretending to admire the lovely surroundings.

"Aisier t' catch a fish wit' yer hands," one of the girls says saucily, "than t' get caught an' flogged fer walkin' the roads wit' a fishin' pole."

"Or worse," the other one says.

The girls are sweet, reminding Red of his sisters and their friends when they were younger, playing innocently in the endless stone-fenced fields of Inis Meáin.

"Ya have a good p'int there," Red says, knowing no one in Ireland, no one rightly belonging to Ireland that is, is allowed to catch fish from the country's abundant rivers. Such luxuries are reserved by British law for English landlords, their families and friends.

"Many Redcoats 'round?" Red dares to ask. "Besides them two on the bridge?"

"Nah. Just them!" answers one of the girls. "They were by our home last night, though, accusin' our fadder o' cuttin' down a hanged man back on the road outside town."

"Aren't they always t' our doors, my ladies, aren't they?" Red says with a little laugh.

"Wish they'd go home out of it," one of the girls says.

Red nods in agreement, saying nothing while scouring the area with his hand above his eyes to block the sun's glare. Taking advantage of the girls' knowledge of the lack of soldiers in the area, he figures it's a good time to continue the long journey home with Brendan and Bolg.

"Alright, my ladies," Red says in a mocking English drawl, "my carriage awaits."

Both girls titter.

"Yer a grand laugh, sure," one of them says.

Red nods, acknowledging their appreciation of a bit of *craic* (fun).

"I bid ye a grand day an' good luck wit' yeer fishin'. An' just in case, here," Red says, handing them a gad holding three large trout he'd caught back at the spot where he, Bren and Bolg rested for the night.

"T'anks, Mister!" they both say, excited. "We're sisters. Can ya tell?" asks the tallest one.

"An' more lovely than Queen Maeve, herself, I might add," Red says. "Clancys or Caseys?"

"How'd ya know, Mister?"

"I don't," Red laughs. "But I knows me country an' what names belongs where."

"Caseys," they both say at once. "We're Caseys."

"Well, Mrs. and Mrs. Casey," Red says with a bow, cap in hand, "as I said, my carriage awaits."

"There's no carriage, Mr.," the shortest girl says.

"An' we're Misses, not Missuses, t'anks very much," the taller one says in her best English.

"Well, someday ye'll be Mrs., I've no doubt," Red laughs, "as beauty such as yours'll have the men proposin' marriage at yer doorstep in no time."

"Mam can't wait fer the day, she's always sayin'," the tall one says, laughing.

The girls follow Red back over the bank and onto the path where they thank him again for the fish.

"Ye should hide them fish," Red warns, "'fraid ye get caught."

"We lives on this side o' Carrick," the youngest girl says. "So we don't have t' cross the bridge an' pass the soldiers," one says.

"We'll hide the fish under one of our dresses, anyway" says the other. "in case one o' 'em decides t' leave their post. Mammy and Da will some glad t' have these wit' our tea this evenin'."

"Smart girls," Red says. "Alright, enjie yer meal," he says while heading in the opposite direction.

He has a closer look at the surrounding area, far and wide, and decides it's safe to retrieve his brother and horse.

Red and Brendan set out on Bolg again for seldom-used paths. Hours later, stopping at a river near Spanish Point, on the west side of County Claire, the men meet a piper named Michael Galvin.

"Ye'll be safe here," Galvin Says. "The few English soldiers that were 'round have been called away t' help ease the risin' tempers o' the protestors in Dublin."

The Spanish Point piper invites the men to his home where they enjoy drinks and tunes. Red passes around his canteen, what's left of his poteen. He even relaxes enough to take his own whistle from the bag slung across Bolg's back, joining Galvin in a reel or two. The friendly stranger's daughters are gifted, entertaining a kitchen full of family and neighbours with powerful, assured voices.

Several hours later, with their spirits lifted and much-needed strength regained from the rest and change of pace, Red and Brendan give thanks to their kind hosts. Brendan has taken a fancy to Galvin's oldest daughter and goes out of his way to try and charm her upon their leave. Red coughs to get his brother's attention and soon grabs him by the arm to remind him the dearness of their time.

Outside the family's garden wall, Red helps Brendan aboard Bolg before mounting the horse himself. Guided by the light of the moon, they head off along coastal trails, towards home. Before dawn, they arrive in Doolin. Brendan finally has a chance to stretch out and get proper rest in Red's boat. Moonbeams shining on Galway Bay guide them in the currach on the fast-moving tide past Inis Oírr and into False Bay before reaching Inis Meáin.

By the time Red and Brendan safely stow Red's boat and take the long way, over countless walls of perpendicular rocks and narrow roads, it is half-past nine in the morning. A crowd is gathered at Houlihan's home. They've been there, on and off, for the past few days; taking turns keeping the widow Houlihan company. Mourning the news of Ellen's death, or disappearance, has become a community event. They won't know the full story until Red bothers to divulge the gory details to his mother, if ever. The loud keening on the part of some of the women in attendance has been enough to keep British soldiers away. They have little to say when it comes to the way the Irish mourn the loss of a loved one.

The war in America is much of the talk amongst the company congregated at Houlihan's and all hands are grateful for it. English troops are scarce on the island and those there couldn't care less about one murdered Irishwoman nor those who mourn her.

Red never stays on Inis Meáin long. His mother's friends and relatives are shocked to see him with Brendan, their tall frames bending to get in the doorway of their childhood home; in its third or fourth incarnation, having been toppled and thrashed by British soldiers on occasion over the years. The family's company begins offering sympathies over the loss of Ellen, but Red hushes them with a wave of his hand. His mother takes him by the arm, guiding him to sit at her little, wooden table.

"Edward, *a stor*," she says in a crying whisper. "Where's poor little John?"

"Safe, Mam," Red says. He hauls his mother close and puts his mouth close to her ear. "With Aunt Mah-ree, Mam. Safe. You'll see 'im before long, ya need never worry. He's a wonderful smart lad, Mam. Big an' strong, too, for a b'y o' five. You'd swear he was seven or eight, the size of 'im."

Red doesn't trust another soul in the room. Not even Brendan knows John's whereabouts. Red's not about to threaten his only connection to Ellen - his sweetheart. His love. He kisses his mother on the cheek, nods to the gaping crowd with their expressions of disappointment. Their necks are still stuck out and their ears straining for a chance to catch a bit of gossip. Red gently pats Brendan on the shoulder.

"This young man could use a rest, if ye all don't mind," Red says, looking around the tiny room. He throws a large salmon on the table and the crowd sounds in awe. "Mam's alright now. Ye can go back t' yeer homes. T'anks fer lookin' out t' her."

When the crowd leaves, Red tells Brendan and their mother some of the events of the past few weeks, and how he, too, is considering moving away from Ireland. But doesn't say where.

"I'll be back, Mam. I have t' go check on John, ya knows that, right. I'll be back, " Reds says in response to his mother's look of worry.

"Of course, me B'y, " she says. "Of course, *mo ghrá* (My

Love).”

“Make sure this one lies down for a week or so,” Red says, looking at his mother, then nodding in Brendan’s direction at the table.

Mrs. Houlihan’s eyes are dark and wet from a lifetime of worrying and crying. She gives a little toss of her head in response to Red’s order, as if to say she’ll do her best but Brendan’s liable to leave again the next day. That he’s beyond her control.

“What about what we talked about, Neddy?” Brendan says quietly, as if their mother can’t hear. “What if that British bastard is sent away from Ireland, altogether? We’ll never get a chance to avenge poor Ellen’s death.”

Red turns away from the door leading into the garden, walks over to Brendan and bangs his big fist on the table.

“We?” Red roars. “There’s no *we* in this!”

Brendan hangs his head, his eyes shooting quick glances at their mother back sitting and crying in her chair by the hearth.

“Do what I told ya t’ do, Bren!” Red continues. “Rest! Stay here long as you’re needed. Keep yer gob shut! One word, remember, t’ the wrong ears ‘round here, or anywhere, an’ the peelers will be here destroyin’ Mam’s house again. Is that what ya wants? Is it?”

“No, Neddy,” Brendan says quietly, afraid of further upsetting their mother. “I just t’ought I’d help ya, that’s all.”

“Forget it,” Red says quietly. “T’anks fer wantin’ t’ help me, but I’ll decide what’s best in this situation. Ya can’t afford t’ get into more trouble. Stay here an’ rest. Size t’ings up. Listen t’ every conversation. Learn. A silent mouth is sweet, right Mam?” Red gives their mother a grin, tossing his head toward Brendan.

Red lugs his currach into the pounding surf and tumbles into the boat. He grabs the heavy, square oars, heads back to Doolin and retrieves Bolg from a friend's pasture. He takes paths along the Aille River through Doolin and Listoonvarna. County Claire is beautifully-sad to Red, reminding him of places where he and Ellen often stowed away and made love, in the hidden crevices of the deep canyon. In the evening, Red rides into Galway. To Aunt Máire's. To John.

On his way, Red lets his thoughts drift to things written in the letter from his good friend, Andy Hunt, in Newfoundland. The woods. Trees. Free? Free to chop and saw? To cut and use any way you choose? And free? Can't be true! But why would Andy say if it if it weren't true? Hard to imagine, is all. Red sees John and Ellen playing and laughing and running towards his open arms in a big meadow above the shimmering sea. Local men pass him by, axes slung over their big shoulders, singing while they guide dogs, goats and horses towing their hard days' work of sawed and limbed logs on carts to be used however they wish. Women and girls talk to one another over clean, white sheets flapping on thin rope strung from one tree to another. Other children run, jump and skip, singing as loudly as they can. All this wonder taking place without fear of ridicule and chastising from ignorant English soldiers bearing arms.

The sunlight is warm on Red's cheeks as he bobs along on the back of his ever-faithful companion, Bolg. Leaving the fairly smooth path of a meadow, Red and Bolg enter a wooded area devoid of full sunlight as they'd both experienced and enjoyed just moments ago. The ground is rocky and uneven - not the most comforting for either man or beast. The shadows of large trees remove much of the sun's warmth and Red's thoughts quickly turn back to the present. Ellen is gone! Gone for good! And there will be no such dream-come-true: of Ellen and John smiling, laughing, dancing and running towards him in an unspoiled, peace-filled meadow surrounded by kind folks at ease. A crow perched upon a dead tree branch caws loudly, quickly stealing Red from his thoughts and mixed emotions. He smiles and tosses his head, taking the crow's interruption as a good sign.

"At least I'll always have John," Red says, patting Bolg.

# CHAPTER ELEVEN

## *Life after Ireland*

*Mid-September, 1778*

Instead of dealing with the pressure of running and hiding from the British Army for his recent actions of retribution in Ireland, Red decides it is time to leave.

John Houlihan, Red's son, who'll soon be six years of age, receives vital tutoring from both his Da and Aunt Máire. For the child's safety it is best he uses a different name, altogether. Morning, noon and night, during the two weeks before Red is to leave, John is instructed and quizzed until stating his new identity becomes second nature to the child.

"What's your name, Boy?" Red asks John in a stern, mock-English accent.

"Patrick, Sir!" John responds.

"Patrick what?"

"Patrick Pryor, Sir!"

"How old are you, Patrick Pryor?"

"Seven, Sir!"

"Small for seven aren't you, Mr. Pryor?"

"Yes, Sir! That's what everyone says, Sir!"

"Where are you from, Patrick Pryor?"

"Cavan, Sir!"

"Who are your parents?"

"Richard an' Norah, Sir!"

"Where are they?"

"They died, Sir!"

"How did they die?"

"They got sick, Sir!"

"And you didn't get sick?"

"No, Sir. They sent me t' live wit' me aunt."

"Do you like it here in school, Mr. Pryor?"

"I do, Sir!"

"Good! Maybe you'll make something of yourself one day and serve the King of England?"

"I would like that, Sir!"

This drill has been practiced over and over, and John has his answers memorized better than Red or Aunt Máire could have imagined.

"Remember, Mammy said I could be a writer or teacher when I gets older because o' my good rememberin'," John says.

"Oh, I knows you'll make a fine writer or teacher someday, John," Aunt Máire says.

"Maybe even both," Red adds.

Red does his best to explain his leaving to John.

"You'll do well in Aunt Mah-ree's care, Son," Red says, holding John close. "Remember, John, I'll only be gone 'long as it takes t' set us up a proper home fer us in Newf'undland."

"Is it far away as Cavan, Da, where ya went before?" John asks, keeping his head buried in the warmth and comfort of Red's shirt.

"'Tis far away, Son, 'Tis." Red answers, choking a little on his words. "Da an' Bolg have t' ride all the way t' Cobh, in Cork, first; then we'll get on one o' them big ships an' sail 'cross the ocean."

"Can't I come wit' you an' Bolg, Da? I won't take up much room."

"More than anyt'ing, John, I wish I could take ya wit' me, but yer better off here 'til I gets meself straightened away in Newf'undland."

"Da?"

"Yes, Me Son?"

"Is Mammy goin wit' ya, too?"

Red bursts into great sobs of sadness and hauls John even closer to his trembling body. Aunt Máire can no longer control her emotions, either. She holds her hands to her small face in an effort to conceal her gasping at the child's innocence. When she exhales, her lungs send out a mournful cry which startles little John.

"Mammy will always be wit' me an' you an' Aunt Mah-ree an' everyone she loves, John," Red says, trying to sound as brave as possible.

"Is she wit' the angels, Da?"

"She is, Son."

"Maybe Mammy's an angel, too, Da?"

"'Deed she is, Son. 'Deed she is."

"Then she'll watch o'er me when yer gone, Da."

"Of course she will, John," Red says while slowly removing his grip from around John's little body.

Aunt Máire brings a cup of fresh goat's milk to table for John in an effort to make the parting of father and son seem more bearable.

"T'anks, Aunt Mah-ree," Red says.

He stands and hugs the old woman, then bends over to give John another last kiss on the head before leaving.

"*beannacht agus ádh mór* (Goodbye and good luck)," Aunt Máire says, giving Red a soft hug.

"*go raibh maith agat* (Thank you), Aunt Mah-ree," Red says. "*d'fhéadfadh Dia a bheith leat* (May God be with you)."

Walking out the door, Red feels no better than when he was leaving Ellen behind, wounded, in the hills.

The increasing tensions in England due to the war in America keep British soldiers extra busy in Ireland occupying larger towns and cities. This helps free Red's passage through areas now less traveled by enemy soldiers. Alone and unnoticed, Red makes his way to Cobh, a port town on an island in Cork City's harbour.

Red boards a ship bound for Newfoundland - a British-claimed colonial island on the eastern side of North America.

"With more storms this time o' year," Red is told by one of the ship's crew, "we're expectin' this crossin' t' take 'bout fifty days, p'raps more."

Prior to now, the farthest Red had ever been at sea is traversing the spans of water between the Aran Islands and Connemara, Galway and Claire. He only hopes Andy Hunt's word of the place, Little Placentia, in Newfoundland is true; that the expected long voyage over the sea will not be waste of time.

Through vicious storms churning up waves mountains high and incessant fog, Red Houlihan and nearly two-hundred more passengers make their way to Newfoundland. After sixty days and nights, the captain and crew of the ship they are traveling on finally spot land. They scour the coastline for a suitable, sheltered bay.

"Lower the main boom!" yells a crewman. "Gather the sails!"

"Drop the anchors!" yells another.

All human passengers stuffed into steerage and still half alive are rustled to deck, put overboard and rowed ashore. Bodies of those who didn't survive the horrendous trip are to be brought ashore and buried once the living are off the boat. Heavy currents threaten to throw the waterlogged vessel battering into the island's natural defenses of perpendicular rock walls, hundreds of feet high in places.

"Mind yer shovin'!" Red yells at a woman behind him.

He stares trancelike at tall, jagged shards of cliff pulled into the ocean by cruel weather and time. The tide is low and shipwrecks can be seen dangling from great granite pillars once part of the toothed cliffs. Red holds his right hand over his eyes and takes a good look around. It's more barren and desolate than he'd imagined. In deep crevices of the rock-strewn beaches flanking either side of the port, Red notices the rotting hulls, gigantic booms and spars of ships - all victims of the cruel ocean now dividing him and John. The long-disputed North Atlantic island seems to welcome no one.

Red's back aches, not only from being beaten off the walls, floors and rails of the half-rotten vessel, but from helping the remainder of the small crew lift and dump bodies overboard on days barely fit to do so. He felt bad for them - the ones who didn't survive the ever-rampant diseases aboard the ship. Some men, delirious from sickness, lost their lives fighting with crew and passengers over a pittance of private space. Regular beatings from blustery weather took care of the rest. Most deceased were wrapped in sail cloth or brin, dealt a quick prayer and dumped into the water a few miles from where the old wooden vessel now lies hove to.

"Two o' the ships that left Cobh the same time as us an' bound fer here never made it at all," A stranger tells Red.

"I'm glad we survived the ordeal then," Red says.

"We're on the eastern side o' Newf'undland's Avalon Peninsula," the stranger tells Red. "Where ya headed?"

"Little Placentia," Red answers, "t' be in the company o' me old friend from home, Andy Hunt."

"There's boats leavin' S'n John's fer udder ports 'round this island," the man says.

"I've no intentions o' gettin' back aboard anudder ship wit'

148

winter about t' begin anytime now," Red says.

"No, b'y! I don't blame ya a bit."

"I plans t' find me new-home-t'-be by trackin' through the wilderness on horseback if I can manage to get a few weeks' work here in Portugal Cove," Red says with confidence. "Ya seems t' know a bit about this place, do ya?"

"Yes, b'y," the man says. "This is me eight year goin' back an' fort' from home t' here. Portuguese fishermen settled this place a hundred or more years ago."

Both men sit on crates on the busy dock to continue their chat and to rest without the sea tossing their stomachs about. Red is surprised to hear both English and Irish accents, along with other brogues he recognizes from encounters with traders from Jersey in the Channel Islands. All hands work, sing and laugh together to make merchantable the year's last catches of cod. Boats, stages and wharves are secured against winter weather.

"'Tis known t' go eidder way here, the weather" the man says, laughing. "Mild or wild."

The absence of total English dominance at Portugal Cove provides Red with rare emotional relief. Several men, perhaps with little to discuss, are quick to bring up the fact the French out of Great Placentia attacked and burned Portugal Cove eighty-two years earlier. They expressively speak of certain scenes as if they had happened yesterday.

"Why in the name o' Jaysus," another man asks Red, upon hearing him speak of his destination, "would a feller want t' go to a place like that?"

Red just tosses his head and grins at the man. He'd like to tell him, and everyone here, how good he has it here compared to life back in Ireland. But he keeps his mouth shut on this one.

"Lookin' fer work?" a tall, skinny man with papers in his hands asks Red.

"Yes, Sir!" Red replies.

"Go o'er there," the tall man says, "t' that ship an' start luggin' those crates from the wharf t' the deck. When ya reaches the hatch t' the hold, tie the rope 'round the crates an' hook the big hook into the knot in the top. Someone else'll take it from there."

"Will do, t'anks," Red says. "From Galway?"

"Connemara," the man says. "But me Mam an' Da came from Galway."

"No trouble t' tell," Red says with a friendly laugh.

"No, I s'pose," the laughs in return. "Now, we'll be hung fer standin' 'round talkin'. Well, not for real. 'Tis not Ireland, t'ank God and 'tis not the English who's runnin' this wharf."

"No?" Red questions.

"Well, 'tis, but you'll scarcely see 'em 'round here," the Connemara man says. "They let us do their dirty work here while they concentrates on makin' more money in the city. Fine by me, t' see n'er Englishman."

"Indeed," says Red. "T'anks again."

"Glad t' help a feller from home," the man says.

Every day for almost three weeks Red works on the wharf, unloading and loading large ships coming to and from England and

Ireland, and smaller ships from other ports around Newfoundland. On days when there is no ship to load or unload, local fishermen are glad for Red's strong back to help lug and cure fish. He's become good friends with the clerk from Connemara, Aiden, and when the time comes for Red to be paid, there are no issues.

"Might be odd t' ask, Aiden," Red begins, "but do ya know o' anyone wit' an old horse willin' t' sell it for a few shillin's?"

"I do," Aiden says. "When me shift is o'er this evenin', meet me here an' we'll go see a man."

That evening Red and Aiden walk the lone road through Portugal Cove, in the direction of the old city, St. John's, and turn down a fenced-in lane. At the end of the lane is a big house. Close by is a stable. An old woman answers the door of the home and invites the men inside. Aiden says why they're there and she opens a tall door to a parlour where her husband sits smoking his pipe.

"Ah, Aiden, me son," the old man says, "come in an' bring yer friend."

"Good evenin', Mr. Murphy," Aiden says. "This is Ned Houlihan, fresh off the boat from home."

"Houlihan, Houlihan," says Mr. Murphy. "I knew a Houlihan, same name as yerself, who used t' make clocks in Dublin."

"Jaysus," Red says, "that was me Gran'fadder."

"Well, now," says Mr. Murphy, "isn't that somet'ing. How can I help ya, Ned?"

"I'm headin' t' Little Placentia, Mr. Murphy," Red begins, "an' after that awful boat ride 'cross the sea, I'd sooner perish this minute than take anudder ship t' me destination."

"So, 'tis a harse ya needs."

"'Tis, sir!"

"I t'ink I can help ya, Ned. 'Long as yer not too picky."

"No, Sir!" Not picky. Just anxious t' get there an' t' see me ole friend an' t' get settled away."

"How's two shillin's, fifty pence fer an auld mere fit t' get ya there? Prob'ly all she'll do is get ya there, but ya never knows."

"That's more than fair, Mr. Murphy. I certainly appreciates yer kind spirit."

"Take 'im out t' the stable, Aiden. There's two auld wans at the end on yer left. Eidder o' them is fine. Take yer pick. I'd accompany ya, Ned, but I'm auld, ya see. I needs t' save me energy, what's left of it."

Red is pleased with the reward for his hard work in this town full of strangers, and is genuinely grateful to the kind man. The old horse seems good enough for the journey to Little Placentia. Mr. Murphy tells his wife to go to the mantle above the hearth and take down a clock. She hands her husband the timepiece. He turns it over and picks at the back cover.

"Have a look at this," he motions to Red.

Red carefully takes the clock from Mr. Murphy and studies it. The old man hands him the wooden back which he has removed.

"'Magine that," Red says, amazed, reading the inscription: "' Edward Houlihan. 1750.' Me Mam said I met him when I was a lad, but I don't recall. He spent his time away from Galway Bay. I'd heared he was a clockmaker, but this is the first bit o' proof I ever see. T'anks fer showin' me, Mr. Murphy."

"Yer kindly welcome, Ned. Now, ya best be goin' before the weather turns on ya. That happens in a hurry 'round here. At least the French, bad as they were, cut a path fer ya," jokes the old man.

Red had battled the guaranteed gales of fall upon the Atlantic and was bruised accordingly. When he'd first arrived at Portugal Cove, his behind was raw with blisters and boils. Now, from the rough traverse overland to Placentia Bay, the boils and blisters have returned. The old horse at times appears more dead than alive. But they've made it. Most bad memories of the sail across the sea are forgotten for now upon Red's realization he's finally reached his destination.

Standing atop a woods path, there it is - the landscape so vividly described in the letter from here to Ireland. From a pocket of his decrepit coat, Red hauls out a crumpled, half-soggy piece of paper to help identify the rough drawing of the peninsular town. Not that he can see it all from his position. With the sun as his timepiece and compass, Red is convinced he's found Little Placentia. All those months contemplating. Planning. Worrying. Wondering. Finally. A dream seen through to its fruition. At last.

Red brings his old mare to a halt to gaze upon his new surroundings. New frost holds everything in its place. On both sides of the narrow path, and as far as can be seen, thickly-branched spruce trees huddle together against the freezing air biting the exposed skin of Red's thickly-bearded face. Tall, wide bunches of grass are pale, twisted and frozen at fifty-degree angles. The dull light of fall dances lazily upon the bright frost clinging to each bent blade of grass. Bent. Not broken. How Red feels. To be upright and vibrant again.

The coastline appears to be about three miles below the point where he and his horse are stopped. The wide valley before them proves the perfect tunnel for the wind breathing salt air from above the incensed green sea. It is sort of like Ireland. But colder. Much colder. The ground seems the consistency of almost-cooled lead, as the old horse's shooed hooves trudge lethargically in place, or back and forth over dips and mounds in the path.

With no real interruptions to his senses, Red notices vivid details of nature for the first time since he was a child. Snow from the night before has melted into tiny icicles now clinging securely to the sturdy needles of the evergreens. A rabbit, half brown and half white, runs and stops. Runs and stops. With quick movements of its tiny lips, it scrapes frost from a wide, low-lying plant. With its buckteeth, it nibbles the plant quickly and chews it even faster. Then, with one paw in front of the other, the rabbit digs and digs. This time it hauls up long strands of grass. Shades of summer green suspended on the dying grass stand in great contrast to the beiges and faded yellows left by the always-quick introduction of fall and winter in Newfoundland. The strands of grass disappear into the little animal's mouth just as hastily as the rabbit vanishes back under the effective cover of forest. The short song of a tiny black and white bird takes Red's mind back to the paths along the old meadow back home where he'd often rode on Bolg. With ease he recalls the relief of getting to the field after carefully navigating the narrow rocky paths along ridges in the mountain passes of Longford.

When Red reaches the flats of Little Placentia, the tide is low. The smell of emptied slop pails is strong. Rugged people in dirty clothes shout songs driving them to work the harsh land with battered hoes and bare, discoloured and sometimes-bloodied hands. There are horses, too, but not overly plentiful, as far as Red can see. His initial instinct is to keep to the right instead of travelling onward down the hill.

Once past a sizeable hill of rock, he notices a lake to his left. It is full of floating vessels, all tied together it seems - safe from the fast-approaching winter, awaiting spring. Big men with sharp axes are busy carving new runners for old sleighs: preparing for the arduous task of lugging logs for all purposes from miles back in the woods on sleds carved from the same forest. Whistling or singing away while they work, men keep on with their business as the stranger either passes or approaches them. Some curse at children in the way. The children, more carefree than he'd ever known his John to be, pay no heed to the crooked men and continue their games of sport. The women, Red figures, are safe from the frost, tucked away in the wooden buildings with smoke billowing from their chimneys. Their homes. All wood, it seems. Just like Andy said in his letter. No mud and rock walls or turfed or thatched rooves.

Wood lies in gigantic piles on both sides of the path and, closer to the homes, neatly sawed and stacked wood stands alone or against the sides of houses, sheds and barns. Land is separated not by perpendicular stone walls like on Inis Meáin, but by long trees limbed of their branches and bark and nailed sidelong to thick posts, also cut from trees. Inside the fences running from the lake's boundaries to great meadows meeting the edge of an abundant forest are cows, sheep and goats. All around the sawdust-covered grounds near the homes are hens, noisy roosters, cats, their playful kittens, and barking dogs. Other great lengths of cut timber stand upright in triangular patterns beside outbuildings and sometimes against naturally-displaced boulders.

*What a wonderful place to live*, Red thinks.

When he asks where he might find Andy Hunt, Red is told he's in the wrong town.

"It can't be," Red says, confused. "'Tis the very same as described in Andy's letters."

"No. b'y," an old man laughs. "Yer not in the wrong place, altogedder. Andy lives o'er there."

Red is relieved. The old man's crooked index finger points above the water.

"Oh, he lives on the other side o' the lake?" Red questions.

"Pond!" the old man says. "'Tis a pond. Not a lake."

"Oh?" Red says.

"Yes, b'y. Shag Pond 'tis called," the old man says. "After the birds, ya know." He's seemingly proud to be educating the stranger. "You'll find Andy on the udder side. Just go back the way ya came in an' keep on yer right. There's just the wan road right t' the end o' Liddle Plazencha. This place, where ye're to now, is Marquise."

"Marquise. Yes. Andy certainly mentioned this place in his letter," Red says. "Alright. Good t' meet ya, Sir. T'anks."

And off Red rides. Wasting no more time. Anxious to see his friend. To get rest.

"If ya hadn't the harse," the old man calls out. "I'd offer ya a ride 'cross the pond in me boat. Save ya time."

But Red is out of earshot and doesn't hear him.

The scene on the other side of Shag Pond is no less busy than the one in Marquise. Perhaps even more so. Balancing on sticks resting on their shoulders, young boys and girls carry galvanized buckets of fresh water from the pond. Two pails apiece. Along narrow paths following the pond they walk slowly, steadily, then off onto other, tighter paths connecting to homes. Inside the many fences of long, skinned logs, giants of men beat horses, cows or, in one case a pack of big dogs, as they haul heavy wooden and iron plows through frosty soil as black as Ireland's bogs. Houses, cut and carved out of the hills of Marquise's dense forests no doubt, puff white smoke which disappears into a thick blanket of fog. Not unlike Inis Meáin in that regard. Not at all.

Everyone Red passes has a smile or at least a curious stare. A few hesitate to half-politely demand a hand from the red-headed stranger. He confirms accents from Waterford and Wexford on Ireland's southeast coasts, as Andy said they'd been arriving in dribs and drabs from those places for the past number of years. Another sigh of relief comes over Red with the realization he's finally made it to Little Placentia. He does his best to avoid divulging details of his horrid journey over the sea. Instead he focuses on asking questions about this place. He misses Bolg. Indeed he does. His guts clench and turn at the possibility of one of these strangers having an English accent. So far, so good. No sign of them. He looks to the sky and misses Ellen, wishing she and John were by his side.

"I seen more meat on Good Friday," says a strong voice from behind cords of large, limbed spruce.

Red dismounts the old mere. He hauls his torn, woolen coat back over his uncharacteristically-thin frame, having spent the past hour or more unloading a horse cart of timber fresh out of the bountiful woods.

"Jaysus, ya waren't pullin' me leg, after all," Red laughs, noticing his old friend coming toward him, arms outstretched for a welcoming pat on the back.

"C'mon," Andy beckons.

Red smiles and gives a light tug on the horse's bridle and the pair follow Andy. Red is too tired to say much else.

They ascend a short meadow of pale-yellow grass. Red ties the old mere onto a tree outside Andy's house. Red notices the back of the home is fastened in places to a thick droke of trees - for extra shelter against damp, cold weather synonymous with Newfoundland, and not entirely unlike the climate of much of Ireland. They enter the one-roomed tilt.

Inside the Hunt's home is warm and cozy. A humming, smiling woman introduces herself as Andy's missus, Patricia. Half a dozen children dance and play in the small room. Upon the sight of them, Red misses Ellen and John again, but his grateful smile hides the deep pain concealed in his heart and mind. Fresh fish and potatoes are frying in a pan on an iron grate above a fire of burning wood. The smell is heavenly. The absence of the odour of fuming peat is obvious to Red, but the hearth made of large slabs of carefully-mortared rounded rocks is clearly the foundation of, not only the home itself, but the family, too. Though, the aroma of wood burning is no less delightful than peat.

"When ya said ya had access t' wood," Red begins. "I'd no idea the amount of it. When ya said t'was endless, I'd t'ought ya were only havin' a bit o' the *craic* (fun)."

"We'll never live t' see the end o' the wood here," Andy says. "Plenty o' peat, too, but why bother?"

After a feed of fresh fish, fried potatoes and two cups of tea, Red fights to stay awake. As he drifts off, he listens to his friend's knowledge of Little Placentia and Newfoundland in general.

"The French were driven from here be the English sixty-five year ago," Andy says. "They used t' call it Petite Plaisance. Great Placentia is just a few short miles' sail around the coast, ya see."

Red's stomach turns again. The English, The last ones he wants to encounter. But he already knew they were here from Andy's letter. At least there are no armed soldiers parading the roads.

"They can be found, not that we're lookin' fer 'em, in several forts 'round Great Placentia, the Jersey side an' a valley town just up o'er the hill called La Fontaine," Andy says. "But the English in them places are too occupied wit' preparin' fer invasion from other countries eager t' get their hands on Great Placentia's large beach just right fer dryin' fish. The outer beaches of this place, Little Placentia, are narrow. Too rough an' dangerous fer landin' large vessels."

Red is too tired to comment or ask further questions. There's plenty of time for that, he figures. Andy's questions about home, and what Red might make of himself one settled here go unanswered, as Red begins snoring. Deep sleep brings him dreams of back home.

The next day is nearly done when Red finally awakes. The journey from Portugal Cove had done him in, although he hadn't felt extra unease during the long traverse across the peninsula of Avalon. Nothing here, he assumes, could ever be as awful as the sixty-day trip he endured crossing the ocean. At sea there were more times than not when he was certain he'd never see land again, let alone feel it beneath his feet. But here he is. And he plans to waste no opportunity learning what he can of this new land and the ways of the *Bay of Plaisance*, as some locals still call it.

To help get familiar with his surroundings, the first thing Red does is walk the length of the town. Heading east he is oddly captivated by the roundness of the rocky hills making up the circumference of the ocean across the mouth of Little Placentia Harbour. Red wonders why the name of the entire bay still has the French put on it by locals but the town, itself, and its harbour's name is spoken and written in English. Two of the rounded hills of rock closest to Little Placentia guard the entrance to a tiny settlement called Little Gloucester; named for a town in Massachusetts, in the United States. Red's friend there was right. The Yanks *did* come all this way for bait. Even to settle.

The early December wind sweeping over the Little Placentia

peninsula from the southwest sends chills down the back of the neck of Red's tattered, knitted coat. In an instant, the winds shift and blow harder still from the northwest - carrying with it light flurries of snow and the stinging, salty spray of the sea. Red hoists the bit of collar which hasn't unraveled from his overcoat, bringing it to the front to ward off the wet snow and the wind's chills now causing the skin of his chest to shiver into goosebumps. Turning his body in the direction of the wind, a small island catches his eye. Must be *Fox Island*. Andy had mentioned it earlier. A good place to shoot birds. While the top of the island is shrouded in what looks to be evergreen trees, its wide, tall edges of limestone shine under the evening's last allowances of light. The churning green sea licks savagely at the solid outer crusts of the little island, sending spray high into the ever-cooling air and across the solid mass of forest it wears as a cap of protection against nature always acting its worst.

*Na Beanna Beola*, Red mutters into the wind. While nothing in comparison to their impressive scales, the colour reflecting off the island's edges reminds him of the Twelve Pins. From many angles at home had Red admired those glistening quartzite, sharp-peaked mountain ranges of Connemara.

When he reaches a long, sandy beach at the end of Little Placentia, Red more closely admires the simple, yet majestic features of the two round hills of rock outside Little Gloucester. Amongst the goose grass not yet felled by frost, two curlews forage for food - the lopping water of the shoreline no match for their elongated, scrawny yet sturdy legs. Nor is prey any match for the quickness of their prolonged curved beaks. They, too, put him in mind of his home island, Inis Meáin. Of Ireland.

Looking farther up and down the beach, Red sees no other curlew. But there are ducks and geese galore. All doing their duty of searching and diving for food in the swiftly-moving waters beneath their feathered bodies. The metallic blue of the ducks' feathers catches hold of the sunlight. Gulls stand, heads bent against the wind which has shifted yet again. This time it blows from the northeast and the added cold it brings is enough to make Red turn his back to the mile-long stretch of water between himself and the rounded hills of rock across the way. The flurries have subsided, but he knows it won't be for long. He'll visit the beach again. What fun John would have here. Maybe they'd even manage a trip across the harbour mouth for tea on that lovely little beach separating the rocky hills. The pointed tops of tall, coarse grass poke Red's knees through the holes in his pants, as he makes his way from the beach and onto the main path leading back to Andy's.

Sizing up the inside of Little Placentia's harbour, it is easy for Red to see why all the town's homes rest in the relative lee of the sheltered inlet - the peninsula's centered highpoints providing protection against the raw winds most always heading off the bay. Despite this observation, plenty of barns and storage sheds free from shelter dot the terrain. In places, according to Andy, a great portion of the town contains twenty and thirty feet of bog, and although it is accessible from a deep beach on the outer sea side, few cut peat. Red already appreciates the abundance of wood offered freely by forests as far as the eyes can see.

Across the harbour is Marquise. Although many houses face the sea, the settlement has the woods at its back. A place to seek shelter, if necessary. And spaces to hide when the past comes around to haunt him. Where he once envisioned himself building his home close to Andy and his family in Little Placentia, the empty coves of Marquise call to Red. Through drokes of spruce and great stands of birch glistening in the evening of the day, Red's attention is drawn to the paleness of meadow after meadow. Sure why wouldn't he make himself a small house over there? The long road between both towns matters not when a boat can take him back and forth to visit his friend as he pleases in a fraction of the time. Besides, as far as he can gather, no one is in ever in much of a hurry in Little Placentia *or* Marquise. That, Red notices, is evident in their easy manner.

And he does just that. It isn't long at all before Red erects himself a sizeable homestead, something to build upon. To settle into. Like most people in Newfoundland, it makes sense for him to live as close to the sea as possible. Where the fish are. His new home in Marquise is nestled in a vast meadow. A narrow, rocky path connects Red's home and garden to the sea. Andy had told him how French armies camped upon these meadows for the fifty or so years they were there - for the same reasons - to be near the ocean and its fish. And for lugging kelp for fertilizer to their gardens of vegetables.

When he's not fishing, chopping down trees or building fences and a barn, Red works on finding materials - crudely assembling forging tools to supplement the few he'd brought from Ireland and those he'd scrounged in Portugal Cove. On both the water and wharves he's made acquaintances requiring and requesting items made of iron. Horse shoes and the small, square nails used to apply them. Hooks and frames for block and tackle. Hinges of all sizes and shapes for doors and hatches. Bigger nails for the construction of fencing, barrows, carts, sheds, barns and houses. Small hoops for dip nets and bigger ones for barrels and wheels. Small wheels for pushcarts and ships' riggings. And bigger wheels altogether for wagons. Plenty of work. Bartering power galore. Perhaps even the odd coin.

The area's center of commerce is situated just across the harbour at Little Placentia. It is there where Red has no choice but bring his fish to English merchants. There'll likely be times it might take all the discipline he can muster not to lash out at them, but he's well-versed in patience. For all England's servants had done to him and his family for generations, his memory is long. His patience short. He reviles their look, their smell, their sound. But hatred has to go. If he is to survive here. Or anywhere.

Sometimes, he takes small orders for odds and ends, and is paid with scraps of iron eventually useful in the making of an anvil and other necessary tools, once he acquires all that is needed to erect a working forge and cooperage. Wrecked ships along the coast also provide a variety of metals.

Comfort exists in the fact the English aren't so much ruling, as running the place in terms of grading fish and lending supplies to fishermen. They employ Irishmen, renowned for their fearlessness on barques, other big fishing vessels, and small boats alike - their untiring ethic to finish what they started - even their brazenness when it comes to not giving into the Americans so often sure they'll get away with paying the lowest prices for bait loaded into their large banking ships. The Irish will stand for none of that. English merchants, seeing every shilling collected will never touch the hands of fishermen like Red Houlihan and Andy Hunt, may even be a little grateful. Especially that they, themselves, don't have to barter and fight with brash skippers and seamen from the coastal colonies of America.

Red is literate. Merchants stand no chance of ripping him off. *The Big Red-headed Brute*, as he is known to those who talk behind his back, doesn't think twice of clouting someone for trying to wrong him. In that regard, he is no more bothered in Newfoundland than he'd been in Ireland. If only Ellen was here to see.

The Irish do the work and the English plunder and prosper. Not an old idea, as far as either side is concerned. But it is a healthier pact than anything the Irish have ever known at home. And with the Irish fond of having big families, it will only be another generation or two before the English will be outnumbered. Out of place, altogether. One day, please God, they'll leave Little Placentia to bother people elsewhere. God knows they can always go back to Ireland and join their mates with the security of England at their backs.

In an inlet of the sea, between Little Placentia and Little Gloucester, is The Sound - a deep-water fiord where Red hand-lines cod as big as those caught anywhere in the world. In places around The Sound, scattered remnants of scuttled French battleships of long ago reach barely above or just below the water line. Depending on the tide and time of day, large spiked hulls and sharp splintered pieces of decks, some with cannon still attached, are visible. A sure threat to sailors unfamiliar with the location of wrecks and the area's deadly measure of currents. Once used to this, it is a relatively easy life for Red. That compared to working the open sea in Galway Bay, the sea breaking ferociously, far-flung from the shores of Inis Meáin.

"The wooden boats built an' used here are a lot heavier," Red says to Andy. "But I s'pose they have t' be t' suit the rough seas. Better than the raw hide currachs we uses at home."

Whenever possible, Red gets drunk. Obtaining spirits in secrecy from the American colony sea captains is a deal which always ensures the English merchants never get all they feel they are owed. Red is scarcely without a cellar full of booze. Not that every single drop is bad to Red. A little satisfaction comes from it. Or at least means to escape awhile when the reality of his horrid past creeps upon him. His thoughts often knock him down, taking him by surprise like rogue waves and washing away any remnants of common sense he might have managed to retain. While most attempts to drown unpleasant memories fighting to control his mind only intensify his hurt and irrepressible madness, the drinking continues.

At sea, especially, a steady nip of alcohol fends off the ever-present chill of saltwater spray and bitter winds. But mostly the bad memories. And they become more plentiful each day. Every time, before the cork is plucked from a bottle, the anticipation to avoid reality is high. But the moment the alcohol takes over, he wishes he hadn't touched the stuff. But then it is too late. The look on Da's face as he was dying becomes clear and bright. No turning away from it. The smell of freshly-spilt blood is as horrid as the moments he'd been there all those years ago. The split second he'd had to lay his hand on Da's head before fleeing the battle scene plays over and over, as he stumbles around the fields of Marquise. One moment he wonders where the ancient Irish war cries come from. The next he knows the voices are his own. But there is no turning back once the booze takes hold. The remaining heat in Da's head burns Red's hand. Or at least that's how it seems. He tries re-entering the battle scene and doing things differently. He would have, should have taken poor Da. Taken him from that place of misery. Taken him home. Made him better. But in reality he did none of that. There was no time. At least that's how his sixteen-year-old mind thought at the time. He'll never forgive himself for allowing his father to die. *Perish*. That's what he did. Perish. Not die. And to make matters worse, Da died not in the company of his family or in the quiet of the home he'd built with his big, strong hands. But on cold ground many miles from home. Surrounded by dead and dying comrades. And English soldiers.

Red curses the bottled spirits. The American sailors for making it part of the bargain. But mostly he curses himself for putting it to his lips in the first place. These drinking episodes inspire so much guilt, and the only way to clear his mind, so he thinks, is to start another bottle. Then it becomes Ellen's turn to haunt him. The one who'd abandoned her. He feels her touch. Her kiss. Hears her soft, but sure voice echo all the regrets he's had since she was last in his presence. Another swallow. John's cries throughout the night. The questions in the morning. Every morning. Another bottle.

Nearly two years have passed since Red first arrived at Little Placentia and made his home and new life at Marquise. The notion that he could function any longer without his son becomes pure foolishness. Upon the sea six days a week in the early mornings, Ellen's ghost appears to Red through the thick fog. His reflection in the deep, dark water while hauling in his fishing line often turns into Ellen's face and body. She is falling backwards. Her mouth is open and she appears to be screaming, but no sound comes from her. When sudden storms fall upon the sea, it is Ellen's voice which guides Red through vicious white caps and inflamed waves to the coast where his rowboat can land upon a beach or around Little Placentia's Pond Head and enter the safe lee of the harbor. On Sundays, when Irish Catholics choose praying over fishing, Red settles for the solitude of his home or, when the winter passes, long walks through the hills where he, somehow, feels closer to Ellen and John.

In the evenings, through paths of the thickly-covered spruce hills of Marquise, Red continues to seek and provoke the devil in himself. He'll fight with it, and later relay his drunken encounters to friends, as if it were all true. He is a mess, never to get over the sound of the musket ball hitting Ellen's back. He misses John deeply and can no longer be without him. He takes passage on a St. John's-bound ship and from there finds his way back across the sea to Ireland.

# CHAPTER TWELVE

## *Life Anew*

By the spring of 1792 a lot has transpired in Red Houlihan's life. His new wife, Catherine, and their children, Bill, Edward Jr., Paddy, Ellen, and John set sail for Newfoundland.

"I'll be somet'ing sick, Red Houlihan, on the sea fer two months," Catherine says in her soft voice. "I'm wit' child."

"Oh, Jaysus, Mary an' Joseph, yer not!" he beams.

The storms are few this spring and the Houlihans sail into St. John's in less than thirty days. Nothing compared to Red's first trip over the ocean fourteen years earlier. Not to say Catherine wasn't sick half the time, or more. But it could have been worse. Red knows all about worse trips across the Atlantic.

By the end of June, 1792, capelin season, Red and his family are close to being settled away in Cooper's Cove, Marquise - just across the harbour from Little Placentia. Encouraged by friends there, he'd named the cove after his barrel-making trade.

"Sounds better than Blacksmith's or Forge Cove," Red said to his family.

The Houlihans planted potatoes, carrots, parsnips and turnips, same as in Ireland, and there was no end to the fish - cod and salmon from the sea, and several varieties of trout from the many ponds and rivers dotting the bogs and marshes in the hills above Marquise. And unlike back home, in Ireland, chickens had their own little houses, as did any animals Red and his family could afford to keep, thanks to the endless supply of wood from the unrestricted forests. The peace Red and Ellen had once only imagined was now a reality for Red and Catherine.

That September, John decided to put his years of education from the nuns and his experience teaching on Inis Meáin to practice in Newfoundland. He cleaned out an abandoned outbuilding in a nearby field, fixed it up enough with newly-sawed boards and used it for a schoolhouse. To a handful of local children yet too young to take to the sea with their fathers or to work the flakes with their mothers, John taught lessons. He was just twenty years of age and had the rest of his life to help edify the sons and daughters of poor fishermen from Marquise, and Little Placentia if their parents or older siblings were willing to make sure they got to school most days.

At his forge, Red had little trouble boasting to customers about John's worth to the budding communities. Knowing what the young man had been through as a child and the fact here he was now a teacher to a group of children was worth any harmless verbal backlash dished out behind Red's back.

For six years, John found love in a young woman from Little Placentia who met a typical, but no less sorrowful end, dying of consumption. John, too, had the unpleasant experience and perpetual bad memory of digging a hole for the burying of the love of his life. Unlike his father, John had no desire to seek companionship in another woman. They never had children, and John remained married to his books, teaching whatever students were available.

In the last letter Red ever receives from home, in the fall of 1797, Brendan writes how their mother has died a quick, peaceful death. She just went to bed one night and died in her sleep. No noticeable ailment prior. No complaints. The odd pain and a bit of discomfort from tending to her garden, but that was just old age, she'd always said. She had never said much during her lifetime - just sat by the table and prayed for an end to the incessant struggles in Ireland.

"There was a time," Brendan writes, "that Mam would walk the length of Inis Meáin, taking time to gaze across the bay, to America where some likeness of freedom might have existed."

After Da died, it was well known their mother only looked in the direction from where she last saw him off - he and his comrades-in-arms off in their boats to beat England at their own game of killing to clear the way for a sensible future. But, once again, the Irish lost and she never laid eyes on her husband again. Nor his body. No proper burial meant his soul wandered aimlessly.

"On clear nights," Brendan writes, "she prayed for a glimpse of Da's ghost. Perhaps she thought he'd appear in the distance, below the sheer cliffs of the island, in his canvas boat."

Mrs. Houlihan imagined her husband taking one last walk over the wide expanse of rocky shore and up over the hills, between the stone wall fences, and through the door of their home. After seven years she took to the roads and paths no more. Acceptance diminished her dwindling hope and she left the rest to God, as Catholics are encouraged to do.

"A new guard has taken the place of the old here since you left." Brendan says in his letter to Red. "British officers are claiming the prettiest girls or charming them into marriage. Together they have babies. Soon it will be nothing but an Ireland divided over and over until the Irish are no longer Irish altogether. There'll be less trouble this way, I suppose. Mind you, it has no bearing on the tithes we're still forced to pay the Protestant church, nor does it lessen the number of homeless families dying slow, terrible deaths in ditches."

"But that's Ireland an' will always be, like it or not. Ev'ry Irish person knows that," Red says to Catherine.

"Perhaps we could learn to pretend like the rest of the world," Brendan writes. "As much as we know of it, that is. And if it's anything like this, then it is enough to know."

Brendan's letter isn't all doom and gloom to Red. He feels an acceptance, an understanding in his younger brother and one necessary to survive in the land in which Red could not remain. He praises Brendan for his bravery.

"In my heart," Brendan concludes his letter, "there can't be an equal to western Ireland in all the world and I'll stay and put up with whatever there is to put up with."

The younger brother who'd once damned Red for leaving home now praises him.

"Your children," he tells his big brother in black ink, "are truly Irish and no doubt they'll mingle with and marry other real Irish immigrants in your new land. Someday, for centuries ahead perhaps, Ireland will be properly acknowledged and represented more in Newfoundland than it ever will be at home. And all because of people like you who had the guts to leave."

# CHAPTER THIRTEEN

## *Newfoundland, 1799*

Red Houlihan and his wife, Catherine, sit in silence on an old wooden bench in their stable. She lets go her husband's hand, as he gets up and walks to the horse's stall. Stroking their horse's head, Red remembers the old horse he'd bought from the old Irishman, Mr. Murphy, in Portugal Cove upon his first time in Newfoundland.

"The auld mare outsmarted us all," Red says, "an' lived anudder four or five years past me first couple o' years here."

Out of caution and respect, Red didn't work the old mare too hard. The way Mr. Murphy talked about her, Red was sure they'd never make it to Little Placentia. After Red left Newfoundland, the horse became more of a pet to Andy and Patricia Hunt's young ones. Andy could build anything, as Red always said of him, and the old horse inspired Andy to make a carriage for her to haul. It became the family's first form of transportation, other than just a horse. Before he left, Red made iron hoops to secure the wooden wheels Andy put together, and in winter the wheels were removed and replaced with iron runners for easy movement over snow. Red also talks a lot of Bolg. The two had been through so much together. The only thing he wouldn't speak of is the time the horse died.

Red sits on the floor, his back resting against a timber support beam, next to a pile of hay. Catherine knows Red is off to think, to remember. She no longer wonders or frets if the thoughts to consume him will be good or bad. She loves him. Red's mind leaves the present. Catherine lets him be.

On the banks of Ireland's River Suir, a teen-aged Catherine Casey sits alongside Red Houlihan. She is lonely for her older sister not long left for Newfoundland with her husband from Waterford. Though nearly twice Catherine's age, something in her communicates affably to Red's soul. It's Red she looks at when she talks, and her words are continually positive - no talk of the English, of rebellion, of plans for war or revenge - only to be where her sister, her best friend, is. To live. In peace.

Catherine's parents are very old, about forty-five, and their thinking, she understands, is of the old ways. And since the old ways no longer exist, why stay and pretend they do? Not that she expects her parents to get in a big, stinking boat and pray for a safe passage to another part of the world. She dreads the thought of having to stay where nothing ever changes for the good. Afraid of living. Afraid of dying. Afraid. All those things are in her, pouring out of her cool blue eyes reflecting dark ripples of the river showing distorted pallid clouds roaming aimlessly a sapphire sky.

Red is entranced by Catherine's calmness, her beauty. He doesn't understand his feelings. Nor does he question them. He's just happy she came into his life when she did. Her charm catches hold of his every sense and although there'll always be looking back, there'd be no more going back. Back to those hills and paths. Back to sleepless nights, to anger, to planning the next big one.

Red has a surprise for Catherine - he's been to Newfoundland. The calm azure of her eyes turns electric. Still owns a house there. Bluer. And the land it's on. The most dazzling shade of blue ever. He wipes tears of joy from her face and continues divulging his knowledge of the place which, only moments before, seemed an impossible world away; one she could only dream of visiting.

"There's no end t' the land," Red says, "an' no English about, except the merchant who's too busy t' bother anyone. Besides, he's dependent upon the Irish people who makes up most o' the little town not fully settled."

"Sounds like it has the promise o' boundless possibilities," she says.

Her eyes ignite with curiosity. Likelihoods beyond anything she's dreamt of. Red's spontaneous invitation unearths all the yearning she'd conserved, veiled in thought. The once-stifled energy of her eager heart bursts into a smile Red will never forget.

At fifteen years of age, Catherine is almost a middle-aged woman, and to find a chance at love and leaving seems worth any risk. She accepts Red's guilt and resentment over Ellen, and is willing to give him a new chance at love.

"The name. It sounds French," Catherine says of Red's village in Newfoundland. "Marquise."

"The French were there 'til seventy year ago," Red says. "Drove out by the English who'd been attackin' them on an' off since 1692. Mind ya, there's the scattered Frenchman 'round still, but they're too contrary t' befriend ya, much less bother ya."

Catherine says again how she likes the name. The sound. *Marquise.*

"The 'S' pronounced," she says. "Makes it more complete, somehow."

With the permission of Catherine's parents, twenty-six-year-old Red Houlihan proposes to the young woman. Then, Red has another, bigger, secret for his new love.

"You'd never imagine," he says with a grin, "the name o' the town only a jaunt across the water from Marquise."

"Not Little Placentia?" Catherine holds her hands to her face in anticipation.

"'Tis," Red says with a nod and a big smile he can no longer contain.

"But that's where yer sister lives," Catherine's mother says, rushing to grab a letter with the name *Little Placentia* on it.

Catherine's happiness grows a thousand fold. Her eyes like stars on a clear winter's night. The Caseys embrace one another in the middle of their small cottage.

"I s'pose if I'd said no t' yer proposal, you'd never have tolt me," Catherine says, pretending to hit Red on the shoulder.

Ten-year-old John is confused at first, but the obvious joy Catherine brings to his father is worth more than any misunderstandings the boy may have had. Red has always shared every feeling with his son, especially when it comes to the boy's mother. Red continues speaking and singing of his love for Ellen. This makes young John smile, especially when Catherine encourages Red's stories of Ellen.

Red and Catherine have four children together before Red can convince himself it's okay to leave Ireland; to trust Ellen is safely in God's hands.

Red gets up from the floor of their Cooper's Cove barn and sits beside his wife again.

"Catherine, *muh grah* (My Love)?" he asks.

"Yes, *a stor* (My Dear)?" she answers, touching his arm.

"Always know how grateful I am fer the gift yer smilin' face handed me. R*iachtanach caitheamh* (A necessary distraction). I often t'anked the Lord fer that smile, yer smile, when fightin' t' scrape me way outta the darkness which fell upon me when Ellen....when they...." Red fills up with tears.

"'Tis okay," she says with a smile, laying her head of golden-gray curls on his shoulders.

Brendan had grown from an impatient lad into a composed soldier of the so-called peasant secret society - groups using violent tactics to defend tenant farmer land rights for subsistence farming. For nearly two years, beginning in 1784, he'd been heavily involved in physical violence with the Whiteboys, or Levellers, as they were known by British authorities. Young men dressed in white smocks, raiding the properties of landlords at night. If necessary, they killed in efforts to force the British to lift or even reduce government-flared rack-rents, tithe collection, excessive church dues, evictions and other senseless acts used to keep the people of Ireland in a constant state of oppression.

"Da told me tales o' when he, himself, was helpin' plan giant assemblies fer the Whiteboys in Limerick. That was in '61," Red tells Catherine. "But they did their best t' avoid fightin' an' killin', Da said. They levelled ditches surroundin' good grazin' ground, lands taken from the Irish an' rented back t' 'em. Bastards."

Red's father did little more than write threatening letters to landowners, those who'd been given stolen land by the Crown. He told the British that Irish Roman Catholics had no reason to pay taxes to the Protestant sect. Other recipients of such letters included debt collectors, landlords, and occupants of land gained from eviction, demanding they give back farms.

They'd survived the famine of 1740-41 which starved to death three-hundred-thousand Irish people, and with so much land rightfully theirs, Rebel groups saw no reason anyone of their own should be in want of food. Or anything for that matter.

"He was always goin' on 'bout the Penal Laws," Red tells her, "sick to his stomach o'er the fact Catholics were banned from runnin' fer government since the airly 1600s. The Protestant crowd made up laws where we couldn't own land...unless we turned t' their side. Become Black Protestants? Hardly."

At first, when Catherine convinced Red to move back to Newfoundland, he used to get upset easily. He told her it had nothing to do with her, just he was torn between staying in Ireland and re-joining the never-ending fight and leaving. Leaving - what had tortured him before, and what he was afraid might torture him again.

In time, once he'd accepted Ellen was really gone from this earth, safe in Heaven with God and all the Irish saints, Little Placentia and Marquise might be as close to heaven he'd reach while living. Perhaps free from the places of so many bad memories he could reunite on a peaceful plane with Ellen - the freedom there alone, powerful enough to make that dream come true.

In summer, with school out on Inis Meáin, John kept busy at the potatoes. He made boat trips in all manners of weather to Connemara. Mainly to trade bountiful spuds for peat. He'd been teaching in the little stone schoolhouse on Inis Meáin for three years, since he was sixteen. With the same amount of minuscule English presence there, it was a good place to keep the Irish Gaelic language and traditions alive. All words were taught in both Gaelic and English, should students be questioned and tested by unexpected British officers - not that many could make it to Inis Meáin spontaneously. Folks were always on the lookout for strangers, coming and going.

Red never stopped questioning himself, his decision to keep going after Ellen fell off Bolg. Sometimes, it just didn't make sense. He wasn't guilty of finding new love. The confusion. Aching. What kind of a man would leave his country, not completely avenging his True Love's murder? But, mostly, he was ready to establish permanent roots. Even if it meant leaving Ireland.

Before Aunt Máire died, she'd left notes on scraps of paper around her house, barn and in the stable where bits of Bolg's hair and scent remained. She'd had enough sense to send John to a friend's place, to tell him don't forget to remind people his surname was Pryor - a good Cavan name - anything but Houlihan, and to stress the importance of his education. She told him Ireland would always be like this if *he* didn't change how *he* saw the world. There'd be freedom in that, she said.

Red falls asleep, leaning back into a pile of hay. He dreams he wakes in Aunt Máire's barn. When Ellen runs her hand through his hair, now longer than ever, he smiles and says how he loves her.

"I don't want t' turn an' you not there," he says in a whispering cry.

"Ya don't have t' turn, Ned Houlihan," Ellen's voice is slight, but plain. "Keep on goin'. Save our son, *a stor*!"

Red wakes up, full of the usual mortification, knowing the hand on his head isn't Ellen's at all, but Catherine's.

"'Tis alright, Red," Catherine says. "If it were me gone the way they took poor Ellen, I'd wish fer ya t' never stop wantin' t' find me, either."

Red has nothing to say to that.

One day is much the same as the next. The pupils of Red's

eyes widen and his breathing slows. While he'd like to haul the heads off some people for talking, he struggles to understand that foolish element of human nature; that some feel a need to have a say in the business and choices of others, even when they're not an integral part of their lives. He remains calm. It's nothing new, telling lies, saying all is well, to save your rear end. They'd all had to do it and will have to do it forevermore, if things in Ireland never change. Red fears, one day, Ireland's people will simply become British, forgetting they were ever Irish and what the Brits have done to them - their culture and their hard-fought efforts at revolt and reprisal ending up in books and songs the world over and no place else.

Red loved the simple life: fishing in Galway Bay, visiting his mother, family and old friends on Inis Meáin when time and weather allowed, the plain smell of Connemara peat burning in the family hearth and the bits they'd managed to scrounge from the island's endless fields fenced by those inimitable walls of perpendicular rock.

When the time came to pack their few belongings and leave Ireland for good, no one was as disappointed as Red. He'd never let go the mental burden granted him by his final abandonment of Ellen. But the fact they had a house waiting for them in Newfoundland, the one he'd built years earlier and kept up by a neighbour or two since, was a great weight off his tired shoulders. It's not like he had to start entirely anew again. He'd make the house a bit bigger, have it back in order and to Catherine's liking in no time. He'd bragged to his new wife and their children, including John, about the loveliness of the place, the peacefulness. Their enthusiasm, in turn, pushed his erratic spirit along, giving him guts enough to make the trip again. Only this time, he knew, he'd plant roots no one could ever disturb.

# CHAPTER FOURTEEN

## *Newfoundland, 1808*

His tune on the wooden whistle long over, and the story of Ellen's death told to his young company, Red speaks of the shovel he'd used earlier today to bury John.

"The handle o' the spade 'tis worn," he began. "The auld metal shovel, two thirds the size it once was, 'tis the same wan Da made in the forge on Inis Meáin. I was but nine or ten. When it split from heavy use, Da'd cut it down t' even the rough edges. "'Twas used in vegetable gardens an' surely fer the diggin' o' holes out o' necessity an' fear: caves in the mud walls o' ditches while hidin' an' waitin', slowly advancin' t' the next stage o' revolution we wished fer. An' fer the buryin' o' those poor babies killed fer sport by idle English soldiers an' the poor little darlin's left t' rot 'longside paths in the Longferd Mountains, 'long wit' their raped an' beaten mudders an' they left t' die close by - those poor souls forced t' flee from one occupied village t' anudder, just as their mudders, grandmudders, great grandmudders an' beyond had done." Red's voice is akin to a preacher's by the time he's done summing up these examples of misery experienced by the people of Ireland.

"Jaysus," whispers one of the young men. "Me Da never said 'twas that bad 'fore he left Ireland, only that 'twas bad an' not'ing here in Newf'unland would ever be so bad."

"Yer Da's right, me son," Red says. "Yer Da's more than right."

Red had often overheard Da telling his Mother of these and other atrocities committed by the British in Ireland.

"'Twas little wonder Da carried the spade," Red says. "'Long wit' his iron pike, even long after the muskets wit' bayonets replaced pikes fer most."

The spade, with four strips of iron running from the base over the wooden handle to its tip also proved a deadly weapon, if need be. But today it was strictly a digging tool, striking rock after rock, as Red dug a hole to be his first-born child's place of eternal rest.

John was thirty-six. He'd been the school teacher for children from Marquise and Little Placentia for the past sixteen years. Red, nor anyone else, has no clue what caused his son's short sickness and death.

With John's death fresh in his mind, Red can't help but think of Ellen. Aloud, to his company amongst the rolling fields and woods of Marquise, he relives the time he buried his wife, what was left of her. He cries like a baby. His painful, loud sobs and tears wash away any comfort he might have gained from those in his presence.

"I'd give anyt'ing t' be on Bolg again," Re cries. "Ellen's arms wrapped 'round me waist, an' me little B'y, John, oh John, pretendin' t' be in control o' big auld Bolg. Poor Bolg. If only we'd had taken anudder route through the mountains that day, t'ings might have been different. If…" Red's voice cracks with dryness.

Andy Hunt Jr. hands Red the bottle and Red takes a big gulp.

"When they took Ellen, they took me, lads," Red says in a trance-like state, no longer crying.

The young company who'd felt proud of helping Red from

his delirium of being chased by Redcoats are beginning to feel weary again.

"'Tis a wicked dream that's become me life," Red goes on, "an' I wish t' Jaysus I could wake from it. I'll have it 'til I takes me last breath, I s'pect."

Red rambles about how the Brits were always a step ahead.

"...an' that's why the Irish will never own Ireland," he says. "Part o' me always wished I was killed. Certainly, killed instead o' poor Ellen. Those bastards murdered me soul, an' what's left of a man if he have n'er soul?"

Red doesn't look around or wait for an answer to his question.

"The likes of me, is all," he says. "Finest kind one day, an' out o' me mind the next, wit' no way t' tell what's real an' what's not durin' the times in between. I had t' go. Had t' leave. Had t' come back here. Poor little John deserved a chance an' it was time t' stop bein' selfish."

More than two hours have passed since Red began his story, the imaginary chase between him and the Brits long over, his tales told, his mind all but drained.

"Perhaps anudder night, me b'ys," Red says, shivering in the cold, damp air. "An' remember, b'ys, never trust the horns of a bull, the...."

"...heels of a horse," the lads begin to finish the quote they've all heard a thousand times from the mouths of their fathers and mothers. "Nor the smile of an Englishman."

Red smiles as much as he remembers how, as the two empty

bottles on the ground catch the light of the full moon. He and the young men stretch and yawn, helping each other to their feet.

Along the moonlit trail, without a word they walk. They disperse onto worn paths leading to their homes or their small rowboats waiting on the beach. What else could they ask the old man? What else could be said? Surely, it didn't get much shoddier than what he'd told them. But only in Red's mind are things far worse than anyone will ever know.

Red turns down the road going right, his blackthorn stick echoing off the hard ground throughout the still, early morning air to ward off potential muggers or foes. In his mind, there'll always be someone out to get him. His eyes dart from side to side, awaiting a visit from evil. His hand grips tightly the walking stick.

Passing a big barn near a meadow close to his home, Red hears a great commotion. Thinking there might be a big fight in prospect, and never one to turn down a good row, he again tightens the hold on his walking stick. He quickens his pace toward the end of the barn. As he rounds the back corner of the building, nine black cats carrying a wooden ladder approach him at great speed.

"An' what should be on the ladder, but the Divil, himself," he later told listeners gathered in his kitchen.

The Devil is stretched out full length, his hands clasped behind his head. A turn of his tail around one of the ladder's rungs keeps him from falling off. Red is mesmerized by the loudness of the nine cats singing the Devil's own tune.

As this apparition of evil passes, Red fills with tremendous rage at their impudence. He raises his stick, bringing it down hard upon the Devil's thorny head. With this assault, the Devil lets out an awful howl and falls to the ground.

In an instant, the nine cats are upon Red, biting and slashing with their sharp claws, screaming unbearable screams. Red backs up against the barn, fighting for his life. He lashes out with his mighty arms and hands for more than an hour. In his left hand, Red holds a cat by the tail and under his right foot is the neck of another furry savage. He is walloping away at the beasts when a cock crows from within the barn. At this sound, the cats give up their attack. They roll the Devil back onto the ladder, and take off down the road, screaming and hollering in a blaze of fire.

As expected, no one lays eyes on Red Houlihan for the better part of the next month. When he appears, it is much the same as the last time people have seen him, only worse. He is convinced he'd seen the devil and little good it does to argue otherwise.

Red's children are not far away, the way he always hoped it would be. Bill and Ned Jr. made their homes in neighbouring meadows of Cooper's Cove. They share a small boat for fishing and have crops of their own. Billy, like his father, is a fine hand at the whistle and entertains a crowd every Saturday night in his house with his best friends, the Smith brothers, Ed and Bud. Paddy preferred the less-crowded shores and coves of Merasheen, an island almost twenty-two miles long by nearly six wide, northwest of Little Placentia and several miles distant by sail. It is visible from Little Placentia and the meadows of Marquise on clear days. Paddy's in good with the people of Merasheen and managed to get a piece of land there to make his own home. Ellen, Red and Catherine's only daughter, married Ed Fitzpatrick of Marquise and they have four children, with another on the way. Their grandchildren are the pride of Red and Catherine's lives, and how Red wishes his mother was alive and here to see her son with grandchildren of his own.

"'Magine now," she'd say.

It's only now Red truly understands the intense love his mother held for John. Little Jimmy, Red and Catherine's youngest, born at Marquise in the winter of 1793, is a big, strong lad, soon to be fifteen. He is Red's helper and mate while hand-lining cod in The Sound and out on The Reach - that three-mile span of sea between Little Placentia and Little Gloucester that Red first admired upon his first walk the length of the Little Placentia peninsula. Jimmy works just as hard in the family's vegetable gardens, and has his eye on a piece of land in a cove not far from home. When the time is right, he says, he'll have his own home and a family. Perhaps he'll be content to stay on his Da's land in Cooper's Cove.

In the murky light of dawn, sitting on a stump between his woodshed and home, and staring at the dying orange and yellow leaves of a birch tree, the smell of iron from Red's blood fills his senses. He's cut himself with the axe again, this time while carving a cross to mark John's grave.

The smell leaps into his guts and sickness overcomes him. Ellen's arms squeeze the air out of him. He buckles over in pain. His head touches the ground. Ellen's breath in his ear is hot, reeking of booze. She blames him for what has happened. She grabs for John lying in his coffin, but Red keeps his arms in the way. He gets sicker - vomiting till his stomach is empty, hurting. The heat from Ellen's body on his back vanishes, replaced with a cold, sharp pain. He wipes the corners of his mouth and the side of his face with his shirtsleeve, then pushes himself up and kneels.

In the end of the meadow, with fistfuls of dirt and rocks from John's grave, Red screams for Ellen's return. His only true connection to her has died. Red's voice echoes off the hills and across the harbour. Falling on his side again, his boots scuff the freshly-disturbed soil covering the body of his first-born child. When he closes his eyes, he's on the ship, starving, forced to eat Bolg and throwing up the same time. A rogue wave rolls the crowded ship on her beam ends and the big horse rolls over on top of Red. The pungent smell of iron from the blood squeezed from his own head makes him want to vomit again, but he's drained - his heart and soul, too. Empty. He wishes to turn the rotten ship back towards Ireland, to a time not long ago where he never would have allowed Ellen to fall off Bolg to lighten the load, and he'd get her safely to a hideout in the mountains and, when she was well enough, back to Galway, then to Inis Meáin. He would have had a chance at saving his Love. Instead, for once, he did what she asked of him. And in the process lost her. Forever.

During the remaining years of his life, especially, Red often prayed a quick death would land his spirit back in the mountain paths above Galway where he and Ellen would reunite. All their earthly trials and wounds taken to the sea on a new wind. Misery never more to be known.

Morning, noon and night, he heard her weak voice demand, "Save our son." Guilt was to be his executioner - the cold steel pike of constant regret to gouge pieces from his fragile being. Slowly, gruesomely, pitilessly, eagerly, any bit of sense he might have once maintained had trickled from his head while his soul - that thing of inner strength and pride which no person nor thing was said to be able to be take - was but an empty barrel, incapable of quenching all his once-musical heart desired. To fall, lifeless, into the cold bog, his image erased from a world where he's never been understood, his passions ignored, and his image - that of a wild, untamable animal - erased eternally from all memory is his wish.

Faith, long since his enemy, deserved no place amongst the torture and angst of his hollowed soul. His mother's years spent fell forward on her wretched knees on the hard-packed mud floor of her Inis Meáin cottage, reaching for the hand of a god no one knew existed had done Red little good. Taken were most of his family, friends, his first wife and first child. And for what? For him to avenge? Tried, he did, in so many ways. Still, he could not undo the suffering. Yet, he couldn't summons the strength to take his own life - said to be a sin, a sure admittance to hell - to fling away forever the guilt handed him upon secret baptism into a world where useless prayers served only to interrupt perceptive thoughts and plans of potentially-positive action.

He thanked God for the comfort and escape found in the drink.

# CHAPTER 15

## *Newfoundland, 1825*

Andy Hunt Jr. and his buddy, Mick O'Reilly, have dropped by Red's home in Cooper's Cove, Marquise for a visit.

"I'm a very auld man, ya know," Red says. "How come ye'er not wit' the crowd yeer own age? 'Tis Saturday evenin', after all, isn't it? No workin' t'morrow."

"'Tis," answers Mick. "We're not *that* young anymore, b'y," he laughs.

Mick had been one of the young lads with Andy Jr. all those years ago, back in 1808, around the fire up in the meadow where Red divulged the details of his life in Ireland. He and Red had become great friends since. Hardly a night had passed, no matter the season, when Andy and Mick didn't pay a visit to Red.

"Lotsa fish?" Red asks from his cot of new straw and longers skinned of their bark.

"Lotsa fish, yeah." Both visitors agree.

"'Tis one t'ing we'll always have, isn't b'ys, lotsa fish?"

"'Tis," they answer.

"Are ya up for a chune?" asks Andy.

"Ya wants t' play me a chune?"

"No, Sir. We'd like you t' play one, if yer up fer it."

"Sure, lots o' the young crowd 'round here plays the whistle now," Red says, his voice turned raspy quicker than usual in conversation these days. "Why'd ya want an old feller t' play?"

"'Cause *they* don't play the auld style, the way you do, Sir."

"Auld?"

"Well, 'tis different," says Mick.

"Better," says Andy.

"I didn't know 'twas a difference," Red laughs. "Me Da taught me how t' hold a whistle, one he made fer me, an' showed me how t' make the notes when I was just a lad o' about six or seven. I always enjied it...'specially when alone."

"We heard ya play, Sir, in the classroom when John was our teacher, when we were b'ys; that time he asked ya t' come in t' show some o' the chunes ya learned from the Aran Islands an' Galway. We never forgot that."

Red sits up quickly, begins a fit of coughing, startling Mick who's sitting closest to him in the little kitchen.

"Ya alright, Sir?"

Red grabs for the bottle on the table, fills his mouth with poteen, and appears as though he's chewing it. Swallowing slowly, his eyes roll back in his head from the pleasure given by the drink.

"Not a day passes when I don't t'ink o' me Son taken by the Lord," Red whispers of John.

"He was a grand, smart man, yer Son, Sir," Andy says.

"An' a good hand on the whistle, himself," adds Mick.

"When his mudder was killed, we all died in ways we never had t' sp'ak of. 'Twas her who encouraged his writin' an' larnin'," Red says, a little louder this time. "Not me. I was always on the run. Coddin' meself. T'inkin' Ireland'd be free someday...when I shoulda come here, or someplace, before...before 'twas too late. Useless t' sp'ak o' it now, I know."

"We're sorry fer yer troubles, Sir," both men say.

"I know, I know. Comin' over on the boat the first time, I stood out on deck at night, somewhere in the middle o' the sea, an' there wasn't a sound. Half the crowd in steerage were dead or half dead an' the rest sleepin'. I hauled out me whistle, cried fer me dead wife, an' a giant of a whale come up 'longside the boat...the big eye, the size o' me auld store out there in the yard, I'd say, looked right through me. Then come this tune...one I never heared before. But 'twas fer Ellen, I knew, ...me first wife, not Catherine...an', somehow, it took away a bit o' the hurt. I don't know how poor Catherine put up wit' me, the way I used t' get on...especially in me younger years. God rest her soul. God rest the two o' their souls."

Red admits he's spent most of his life wondering why God put him on earth. Especially since Ellen's death. Once so sure of everything, always a plan for him and his family. He supposes he could have, should have, tried to fit in with society. But that would have meant giving up all he was taught to stand for - to be himself, to represent the dreams of his father, to pass those dreams onto his children. Looking back, the confusion should have been obvious because he'd hardly want his children in harm's way. He'd certainly not want to be the cause of it, if something bad did happen. And staying in Ireland meant residing in the way of hurt, as long as you stayed true to yourself and your nation's hidden notions. As long as the British were there, there seemed nothing left to lose. Leaving offered hope. And to be hopeful in the eyes and minds of many at home was to be altogether delusional.

Red looks through the small, glass window of his kitchen, at the graves of John, Catherine, and several of their grandchildren taken by unnamed diseases. He tells his company he's glad he took time to replace their wooden crosses every few years, and he supposes his children left will do the same once he's dead and gone.

Red guiltily wonders if the unexpected deaths in his life were hidden blessings. Had he time to prepare for the shooting of Ellen, would the consequences have been as bad for all of them? Would things have been much worse? Did he learn *anything* from living years in a mad state of vengeance? Acceptance creeps its stubborn way into the old man's once-immovable heart, and the answers lie in his surroundings - Cooper's Cove, Marquise in general, and Little Placentia. He tells them bits and pieces of that day he first found the place, even remembered the rabbit who crossed his path, the first sign of life he'd met here, and the wonderful times he'd shared with his best friend, Andy Hunt - not long dead, himself. How he was glad no other country tried to invade this place while he was here and how it seemed as though the Irish people were safe enough now from English rule; that they could just as well call this place Ireland, too, if they had a mind to do so.

Looking out, above his roughly-hewn table through a thick, round pane of glass - a porthole window salvaged years ago from a wreck in The Sound - it's all there: the meadows, woods, paths to the ponds full of trout, the rocky lane leading to the seashore where his old boat lays crumbling in rot, reminding him of the many seasons spent catching cod, hand over fist, in The Sound and outside Pond Head and The Point on calm days. Or just perched upon a rock or against a tree smoking his pipe, the smells of a treasured forest, the music of the lopping sea, the odd fish jumping. It all summed up

190

what he, and the rest of Ireland, had wanted. Peace. Newfoundland to him equaled peace.

"This place was everyt'ing the letter from yer Fadder said it would be," Red says, looking at Andy Hunt Jr. "An' how lucky were we t' have survived the diseases that took most o' our friends an' their families here o'er the long years."

Feebly, he makes the sign of the cross over his breast, thanking God for the people not yet taken from him, the men in his company included.

After the long whistle tune, Red recalls his happiest times here in Newfoundland: at home, the youngsters playing and singing and dancing out by the door and in the kitchen here where there was never much room, and then when they'd gone upstairs, to bed, when it was just himself and Catherine to give thanks for another day in this wonderful place. And out around the woods and ponds and Little Placentia Harbour by himself. He loved that, too. The solitude.

Catherine got to grow old with her sister and family, her children and grandchildren, sharing both the joys and burdens comprising life dependent upon a harsh land and a cruel sea. Five years ago she died, in 1821. Red tells Andy and Mick the story of how he met her and how he, unknowingly at the time, met a finale to the insanity fed his mind since birth.

"'Deed, I loved her, b'ys," he begins after another full mouthful of poteen. "Just when I was sure I had no heart left, like a bird just learnin' t' fly, me heart flew from its drowsy state. That was the moment I first laid eyes on her."

Still in the throes of mad passion to avenge Ellen's death, Red rode up and the down the countryside, and all the way across Ireland, too, through the roughest of terrain in places, to make sure support was still there for the cause - to get rid of the British. Free Ireland.

Alongside the River Suir, in 1783, after a secret meeting was held nearby, outside Carrick, Red and a comrade from Tipperary were walking and talking. Ellen had been gone five years by that time. Timing. Everything was timing. Not yet. Be careful. Mind your mouth. Listen. Rebel assemblies were getting bigger and so were the number of enemy troops - now that the American Revolution was over.

In 1781, the British tried to conquer Virginia, but a French naval victory outside Chesapeake Bay led to the capture of a British army at Yorktown by the Franco-Americans. After this last crush, Britain lost much of its will to carry on fighting in America. Warfare continued throughout 1782 on a smaller-than-usual scale for this long, useless battle Britain had declared upon its own people eight long years earlier. At last, discussions about the possibility of peace began. The war ended with the Treaty of Paris in 1783, recognizing the sovereignty of the United States. This arrangement wasn't good news to the natives of Ireland. It meant more English soldiers back on Ireland's soil to better continue what they'd started centuries earlier. And there were no signs of them leaving anytime soon.

For the Irish in Ireland, nothing changed. It meant lying awake at night, fingers on musket triggers, waiting for the first shot of the next uprising, meeting in secret places, hushed tones and ears ever tuned for better ideas and signs from those likely to never fight, to run telling plans to the nearest outpost of British soldiers. Many of these traitors were made away with by simple nods. The understanding: *Na bíodh muinín agat as éinne.* (Trust no one). Swift blows to the head when they least expected it, leaving them for the wild dogs and rats. Their families never questioned. Everyone knew it was the Brits, and what was the use of arguing with *them*?

"That fight breathed its last breat' fer me when I saw

Catherine," Red says, this time clenching his boney chest and wheezing, rather than reaching for the bottle.

Switching stories, driven by some urgency, Red divulges details of his first trip to Newfoundland - a guilt, perhaps, for his horse and companion, since Bolg had been such a vital part of his life and survival. Until now, he'd kept the particulars to himself.

"A confession fer ya," Red begins, "in the hopes me auld horse will have forgiven me fer what I put him t'rough an' that we'll reunite when me time comes t' pass."

The sixty-day sail to Newfoundland Red endured from September to November 1778 comprises another sullen layer of his life. He'd spoken none of this to John, Catherine or their children. A man he knew well from a lifetime of planning and fighting in Ireland had connections to several crew members of a ship which made one or two trips yearly across the Atlantic. Red was guaranteed passage - his own bunk and, due to fewer passengers travelling with animals in fall, a stall in the stable below decks for Bolg. He took the risk.

Every few days, storms threatened the overcrowded, soggy vessel carrying close to two-hundred men, women and children. Normally, there'd been more than three-hundred passengers. It was hurricane season. Red spent as much time as possible with Bolg who was quickly growing weary of the vessel's pitching and rolling. Fights with other passengers caring for their animals were common, as Bolg's hay often disappeared. Red would have none of that. The old horse's eyes developed cataracts, and Red was sorry he hadn't left him behind, in Aunt Máire's stable where he'd be comfortable, properly seen to. But his old aunt was hardly able for the responsibility. She'd been good enough to care for little John.

Human waste sloshed through the narrow wooden corridors of the ship's hull, disturbing the senses and stomachs of all onboard.

Disease killed at least forty passengers who were hurriedly dumped overboard for fear of further sickness spreading. Raging winds and the crashing of saltwater poured through cracked and rotten deck boards, the air constantly filled with the wails and screams of vomiting mothers, fathers, brothers and sisters mourning their dead and dying.

Once near Newfoundland's bleak coast, a major storm did its best to force the ship onto jagged rocks protruding from the angry sea. Several crew members were swept overboard, forcefully requiring Red and other passengers to assist with the hoisting and lowering of sails, as well as the maneuvering of the ship's gigantic booms and spars.

Tears made tracks through the dirt on Red's face, as he approached Bolg's stall where the horse usually had his head out in anticipation of his master's company. In a twisted pile of broken limbs, Bolg lay. The livid sea had been too much for the tranquil, old animal.

"Ya weren't supposed t' go this way, me old friend," Red cried, trying to straighten Bolg's broken legs.

Bolg had barely enough energy to stir. His breathing heavily laboured, blood spurted from his battered nose over Red's hands and arms. The master could bring no sense of relief to his timeworn, faithful companion. Red put his arms around the horse's head, kissing him between the eyes - Bolg's glazed, but still-beautiful, knowing, trusting eyes. His breath slowed, and Red knew he had to bring the swiftest end possible to the suffering animal.

Red sought out the sole remaining crew member of the three he'd been introduced to in Cobh, before they set sail. The other two were gone, the man told Red - long since swept from the riggings into the sea.

The distraught crew member said he'd let Red know when the horse was out of its misery. Red swallowed hard and thanked him. A day before the ship managed to get back closer to Newfoundland's coast, having been forced to sail farther out to sea, a calm, cold day allowed Red and other men to drag and hoist Bolg's corpse up from the hold and out over the ship's rail - the boom arm holding the block and tackle for lifting and landing cargo in and out of the ship's hold long broken by stormy weather.

After a few words and a prayer, Bolg was let loose from the rope and canvas holding his large, heavy body. Red fell to his knees, resting both forearms on the rail of the ship. Through tearful eyes, he watched his long-time travel companion disappearing beneath the surface of the conniving sea.

When Bolg was gone from sight, Red said a prayer and thanked God for the many years he and the horse had shared, realizing he would have met the same sad fate as poor Ellen if he hadn't had Bolg's loyalty, great strength and speed beneath him to outrun the Redcoats that long-ago day. Little John, going on six years old, would likely have been taken and tortured, or at least abused and abandoned like so many of Ireland's children. A large bubble surfaced on the green, brackish water, as what was left of the ship's sails were raised high to help put an end to the wretched, sorrowful journey Red still knew necessary.

The ship carrying Red Houlihan and others landed on the south side of Conception Bay, at Portugal Cove, from where many walked four or five miles with their weak, sick and half-starving families to the island's capital, St. John's, to catch other ships bound southwest to Boston and New York. Others sought out relatives and friends already settled on the rocky shores framing the British colonial island.

Red made acquaintances with the locals at Portugal Cove,

staying the remainder of November to help fishermen clue up the fishing season. Aside from his first job there loading and unloading crates from ships, he hauled nets, removed fish and filled small boats with gigantic cod, salmon, herring and mackerel. The fish were brought to the many small shacks built on hastily-constructed, but reliable-enough wharves and stageheads for beheading, cleaning and salting. *Making fish*, they called it in Newfoundland. Poorly dried, thanks to overcast days and little heat from the oncoming winter's sun, the fish was weighed and graded by merchants - Englishmen, whose idea of fairness was, and still is, nowhere close to what hard-working Irishmen, now Newfoundlanders, deemed reasonable. *Only fit for the West Indies*, they were told, and worth little or nothing - lies enough to ensure poor fishermen and their future generations stayed in the black books of merchants the rest of their lives - a system guaranteed to last hundreds of more years, should the downtrodden people never have guts enough to stand their ground.

At first, Red thought he'd ride out the winter in Portugal Cove, but decided to work a while longer, then find a horse fit to take him to Little Placentia - size up the lay of the land, begin a new life.

In the dim light of a lamp fueled with whale blubber oil, Red dipped a gull feather quill into a bottle of black ink. Wet winds off the ocean pummeled the roughly-hewn house where he'd been boarding since his arrival two weeks earlier, as he wrote.

His letter, to Aunt Máire in Galway, outlined details of his first cross-ocean journey, omitting Bolg's sad demise. Instead, he made a fuss out of the few days the sun shone and the nights the water didn't sweep the ship clean. Red professed his continued sense of loss and disbelief over Ellen's death.

"I've often felt her warm hands on my shoulders or around my waist when alone at night," he wrote.

He also wrote to John, for Aunt Máire to read to the boy, explaining his decision to leave and trying to convince him it wouldn't be long before they'd be together again. The Presentation Sisters had educated nuns stationed not far from Aunt Máire's where John had begun began his studies, Aunt Máire said in her return letter.

After almost two years of living at Marquise, Red had land cleared, a solid tilt and store built, as well as a root cellar to cool his root vegetables, keep them from spoiling. Finding another wife was the furthest thing from his mind then. He wandered the hills and valleys, reminiscing Ellen - the last time he looked into her eyes, the life fading from her body, and little John's torment and confusion. He missed his son and could no longer be without him. Red made his way to St. John's and found passage back to Ireland.

While he'd been away those couple of years, the courts in Ireland ruled Red would be left alone should he be found with a family and minding his own business, staying out of the way of the English, and finally complying with their ever-growing rulebooks. But Red knew that was drivel; that they'd try and hang him the moment they found out he was back. There was always someone to find you out, to tattle, someone less happy, a traitor, looking for a boost of energy by robbing people of their contentment. What more could you have asked for on a good day in Ireland? Nothing worse than a *fealltoir*. A traitor. A *Francach*. A rat. Red hated rats. But he had to stay focused on making his way to John, to see how he was doing in school, how he was coping with his fake name - a Pryor from Cavan and not a Houlihan from the Aran Islands - to see if he was as okay as he told Aunt Máire he'd been while Red sailed away to find a reason for himself in this old world.

The war in America had drained Ireland of British troops for a time and those who now ran the place were unfamiliar with Red.

Posters showing poorly-drawn sketches of his face were long blown away, rotted, or taken and burnt by many who knew Red and/or stood for his cause. *Their* cause. This left plenty of room for Red to roam the hills above Galway City, through the Longford Mountains, to ponder again his past life with Ellen.

His harsh exterior was a far cry from whom he really was and who he longed to be someday: himself. He'd sooner play his whistle alone in the woods, or for a few people who'd listen, than to fight for Ireland any longer. Where did it ever get him, anyway? But that was a coward's reply. No, it's was the voice of reason. *Ellen's voice.* The voices in his head bothered him and he put his mind back to the borrowed horse and familiar, beaten paths beneath him, as they carefully plodded through Ireland's immeasurable fields. His shaved face removed his most notable trait - the big, red bushy beard - and his thick ringlets of orange-brown hair once bouncing on his broad shoulders were now cut close to his head. His body was thinner, his sorrow having stolen any appetite his stomach might have desired. Tattered nerves kept dark circles under his deep-set eyes. Should Redcoats have passed him on his long journey home, he would have been seen as a mere peasant and no longer a *kern* - one of the many names the British called lone Irish Rebels. After a few weeks' rest and good food on Inis Meáin, he'd regain the strength and muscle he was sure to need again.

The years to follow in Ireland brought Catherine and four more children. With no indications the British would be leaving Ireland anytime soon, Red and his family ultimately said good-bye to home, forever. Ireland would have to exist exclusively in their hearts and minds, in song and oration. Home would live eternally through tradition and remembrance only.

In the end, Red Houlihan couldn't save anyone, especially himself, left to stumble and crawl, drunk, petrified and alone, through the hills of Marquise. But this, at least, he did unbothered by travesties once dictating his life in Ireland.

Red makes a feeble attempt to grab the bottle on the table. Andy Hunt Jr., now more than a middle-aged man himself, is about to shove it towards the old man, but Red puts up a trembling hand to stop him. He looks out the window to the graves of his deceased loved ones, then lies back on his cot, arms across his shrunken stomach. After a fit of coughing and momentarily fainting, his eyes open wide. He looks around the room, his thin lips stretching slowly across his toothless mouth - almost a smile, something no one here has ever seen on Red Houlihan's face. A rattling chest and a raspy voice pushes out what surely seem his last words.

"*Is fheàrr teicheadh math na droch fhuireach.*"

"What'd he say," Mick asks Andy.

"Better a good retreat than a bad stand."

Red takes a big breath and says no more.

Both men bless themselves and offer silent prayers for the old man. With the sleeve of his shirt, Andy wipes tears from his eyes. He then closes Red's eyes and covers his face with his unravelling woolly blanket. Mick closes off the stovepipe flue while Andy opens the small kitchen window so Red's soul may travel swiftly across the ocean, back to Ireland.

Andy places the wooden whistle on Red's chest, and offers another prayer for his old friend, this time in a whisper. The men put their caps back on their heads and leave the house to find Red's children, tell them their Da is finally at rest.

A few minutes after Andy and Mick leave, a crow lands on the ground outside Red's kitchen window. Cawing at the top of its lungs, it hops frantically. Red's eyes open wide, his arms remain on his chest, his boney fingers entwined in his whistle of juniper.

Red is sitting atop Bolg who is young and stronger than ever. The horse dances with excitement upon the soft, grassy earth at the wonderful sight. It's Ellen. She's as beautiful as ever, holding little John's hand. They're smiling, waving. John cries out, "Da! Da!" Ellen isn't warning their son to be quiet. No danger permeates the air as they descend a rolling meadow towards where Red and Bolg are waiting. Red dismounts his faithful companion and stands, arms outstretched. He hears his whistle blow a happy tune, as the three embrace in song and dance.

"*Tá síochán teacht*," Red shouts. "*Tá síochán teacht*, (Peace has come)." His voice is reverberated in the empty copper kettle on the stove.

A loud, raspy clatter caused by another breath of air into Red's lungs, his last, fills the low-ceilinged room - enough to give him the strength to turn his lips into half a smile.

The bounding crow caws once more, then flies back to the trees covering the hills of Marquise.

# THANKS

To my brother, Barry, who has called from "away" forever, remaining a sound catalyst in ensuring I continue to research and write. His love of family history and his belief in my capabilities inspire me greatly. To my dear friend, Elaine Murray, whose deep love of Argentia and Marquise and her belief in me as both a person and creator continues to motivate me. To my cousin, Cindy Howard, whose friendship and belief in my writing continues to inspire me. To my good friends, Charlotte MacDonald, Danny Poole and Jeff Butt, for their constant interest and encouragement in what I do. To my dear friend, Rudy Barry, whose amazing art as a painter inspires me to be better at what I do. To my beloved friend, Gertrude (Ma) Osborne, for 25 years of support; for accepting me for who I am and for what I love to do, and to her late son, Joe, one of the best friends I ever had and one who believed in me to the very end. To my brilliant wife, Lori, for making time to ensure these pages and covers have been formatted properly, and for making many valuable suggestions to ensure the information presented reads as a story should. To my dear children, Kayla, Emma and Jessie, for their love, patience and support of this often-isolating work. To Collette Kelly for her help with the Irish language. And to the talented author, Anna Reilly, for educating me on how to do this thing on my own. Also, many thanks to my family and friends, and to all who continue to support my explorations into the past through stories and song.

## ABOUT THE AUTHOR

Darrell Duke was born at Placentia, Newfoundland in 1970 to Gerry and Shirley Duke. He was raised in Freshwater, Placentia Bay. He has spent most of his life as a singer and musician, and has been a photographer, playwright and journalist.

An Irish Tale of Leaving is Darrell's fourth book and the first under his newly-formed Stagehead Publishing. His first book, If You Look Closely, You'll See, was published by Byrnt Books in 1999. When We Worked Hard: Tickle Cove, Newfoundland was published by Flanker Press in 2007. Thursday's Storm: The August Gale of 1927 was published by Flanker Press in 2013 and is also available as an e-book. His last two books were acquired by the Cultural Connections Resource Acquisitions' Program of the Newfoundland and Labrador school system respectively in 2008 and 2014. Thursday's Storm was also attained by the University of Maine, the University of Toronto, and is an e-resource book at Cumberland Libraries, Nova Scotia.

Darrell is currently working on his third studio album of original songs. He is also completing a children's book of short stories entitled The Adventures of Crunch and Munch (Vol. 1), as well as a novel recounting events of the 1941-42 saga at Argentia and Marquise, Newfoundland, when the American Government expropriated both towns for the purpose of setting up a base in defense of Hitler's advancing navy.

Darrell lives in Clarenville, Newfoundland with his wife, Lori, and daughters, Emma and Jessica.

Made in the USA
San Bernardino, CA
28 December 2018